BERLITZ

SOUTH AFRICA

By the staff of Berlitz Guides

How to use our guide

- All the **practical information,** hints and tips that you will need before and during the trip start on page 106.
- The **introduction** on page 6 gives an appreciation of South Africa and its people.
- For an overview of the country's **history,** consult the chapter A Brief History on page 14.
- South African **cities** and **places of interest** are described between pages 21 and 90. Our own choice of sights most highly recommended is pinpointed by the Berlitz traveller symbol.
- **Sports** and **leisure activities** are described between pages 91 and 95.
- A rundown of suggestions of **purchases** to look out for is on pages 96 to 99.
- **Entertainment** in general figures between pages 99 and 101.
- Finally, the pleasures and possibilities of **dining out** in South Africa are covered between pages 101 and 105.
- The **index** on page 127 gives place names occurring in the guide.

Although we make every effort to ensure the accuracy of all the information in this book, changes occur incessantly. We cannot therefore take responsibility for facts, prices, addresses and circumstances in general that are constantly subject to alteration. Our guides are updated on a regular basis as we reprint, and we are always grateful to readers who let us know of any errors, changes or serious omissions they come across.

Text: Ken Bernstein
Photography: Erling Mandelmann
Layout: Doris Haldemann
4 Cartography: 🌐 Falk-Verlag, Hamburg.

Contents

Picture, pp 2–3: Cape Town

South Africa and the South Africans

Here is Africa on a silver platter, the call of the wild at the end of a superhighway.

After a hard day's trek, as birds of outlandish hues race the sky-high scarlet sunset, the traveller can expect a hefty steak and salad and a bottle of good local wine. Air conditioning and colour television are optional. All the conveniences of contemporary civilization are close at hand— telephones that work, express dry-cleaning, bulging supermarkets and book-shops. And no matter where you go, from mountain lodges to lazy beaches to boom towns, you can drink the water from the tap.

But the Africa of fiction and dreams is all around you. In Kruger National Park alone, 122 species of mammal and 422 of birds are protected from

man but not pampered. Even if the leopards or lions should elude you, it's difficult to miss the hordes of elephants, forests of giraffes, graceful bands of zebras. And beyond the game parks, along ordinary highways, South Africans are accustomed to the sight of antelope, ostriches and freelance monkeys. *Do Not Feed the Baboons* signs are as common here as *Keep Off the Grass*.

With an area bigger than California and Texas combined, South Africa calls to mind the same feeling of wide-open spaces. And some of the sights are similar: spectacular coastlines, orchards and vineyards, moody deserts, cities with the glossiest skyscrapers, and suburbs of long, low, white houses smothered in flowers.

In full flower: garden terraces at Union Buildings, Pretoria; off-duty gold miner wears regalia at tribal war-dance for tourists.

It's a big country. Filling stations and general stores can be so far apart you are loath to pass one by. And when you stop, the villagers will eye you with friendly, open curiosity. "What do you think of South Africa?" they ask, hardly daring to blink until the answer is heard.

Setting aside preconceptions, your judgments of South Africa are likely to be as varied as the scenery and the population. It's hopeless to generalize. Consider half a dozen typical citizens: one is a post office clerk with a harsh Afrikaans accent, stoking the charcoal for the beloved *braai* (barbecue). Another is a frightfully British-sounding woman in a white hat, playing bowls on a fanatically trimmed lawn. The Zulu farmer tilling the parched soil lives in another world; his cousin who digs for gold beneath Johannesburg, quite another. The bank teller, classified as "Cape Coloured", thinks in Afrikaans. The Indian entrepreneur in Durban speaks a clipped English. All are natives of the same South Africa, members of a mosaic of peoples making up a world of differences within one land. How they all get along together is a matter of great concern, which has made this one of the world's most controversial countries.

The rich diversity of the population extends to almost everything else in South Africa, natural or man-made. The trees are fragrant pine and eucalyptus, stately palm, and the lonely baobab. Flowers of the most romantic extremes flourish at one altitude or another—native protea, heather, orchids and bird-of-paradise. The architecture is quite as various: "beehive" huts like tropical igloos, rondavels with conical thatched roofs, Cape Dutch mansions all in white, and skyscrapers well worth a second glance.

On a direct flight, a jumbo jet travels from London to Johannesburg, about six thousand miles, in slightly more than 11 hours. South African Airways used to take much longer on this route, since black African countries, in one of the more tangible gestures of protest against South Africa's official racial policies, forbade SAA overflights. Now, however, overflying is happening and, with the process of reform taking shape, the ending of sanctions and the likelihood of an interim

Indian Ocean surges ashore near busiest port in Africa, Durban.

government in sight, many international carriers are making direct flights to the country.

Since the late 1940s, when the policy of *apartheid* (separateness) was codified, South African governments have pursued the separate development of the nation's racial groups. This involved the mass removal of citizens to new housing areas, a ban on intermarriage, and segregated schools, hotels, railway cars, public toilets—even park benches. But many of the restrictions have since been eased, and in 1990 the government opened a dramatic new chapter, unbanning the African National Congress and freeing its imprisoned leader, Nelson Mandela.

Less than one in five inhabitants of South Africa is white. The majority of the population —two out of three—is black, belonging to a number of nations or tribes, the biggest of which are the Zulu, Xhosa, Sotho and Tswana. Just over ten percent of the population is classified as Coloured, meaning of mixed race. Another 3.3 percent is Asian, mostly the descendants of immigrants from India. Incidentally, white South Africans strenuously object to being considered mere settlers or immigrants in Africa, for their roots go back more than three centuries to the foundation of the Dutch station at the Cape. With them, the Dutch language was introduced, and from it evolved Afrikaans, mother tongue of most South African whites (and most "Coloureds", as well). But nearly 40 per cent of the whites are native English-speakers, and English is understood everywhere.

South Africa faces two oceans (the Atlantic and the Indian) and five countries: Namibia (formerly South-West Africa), Botswana, Zimbabwe, Mozambique and Swaziland. An 11,700-square-mile "blank" inside the map of South Africa contains the independent Kingdom of Lesotho, formerly Basutoland. Other "islands" scattered within South Africa are assigned to black homelands (such as Transkei and Venda), which have attained or are being groomed for the status of independent republics. Questioning South Africa's motives, almost all foreign countries have withheld diplomatic recognition from this innovation in nation-building.

Though the map of South Africa is riddled with these perforations, the country is securely held together by European-class communications.

The roads are good; many are first-class by any standards, including some handsome motorways. Domestic air services link all the sizeable towns. And the railway network ranges from the quaint to the super-luxurious.

You can see South Africa by a combination of hired

Galloping feather-dusters: Little Karoo "jockeys" race ostriches.

car, train and plane. Or hire a caravan (trailer) and take your hotel along with you; the caravan parks, very well equipped, are often set in admirable locations. Alterna- **11** tively, abandon the driving and the decisions and join an organized coach tour. It's a question of available time and your taste, but you'll want to strike a balance between the cities and the countryside, between culture and nature.

Most foreign visitors arrive by air, at Johannesburg. A wheeler-dealer city of skyscrapers, it's literally and metaphorically built on gold: those sandy little mountains surrounding the city—a bit too symmetrical to be real hills—are slag heaps from the original gold mines.

Less than 40 miles north of Johannesburg lies the republic's administrative capital, Pretoria. It's easily as pleasant as any national capital on earth, but even more so in the spring when its thousands of jacaranda trees celebrate in flower.

Way over on the Indian Ocean, the city of Durban, Africa's biggest port, is also a beach resort with spicy cosmopolitan overtones. Look for the rickshaws pulled by Zulus in full regalia!

Beautifully packed between the Atlantic and that unforgettable landmark, Table Mountain, Cape Town is known affectionately as the "mother city" (founded 1652). Few would argue: this is the fairest of them all, even though the tycoons from Johannesburg find the pace too relaxed.

Within easy reach of Cape Town is one of Africa's best-known natural attractions, the Cape of Good Hope. The Portuguese explorer Bartholomew Dias negotiated this treacherous turning on the discovery route to the East in 1488, only to succumb to a classic Cape storm 12 years later. You may see it in a tempest or on a beguiling summer day, but whatever the weather, this "end-of-the-world" cape seascape makes for high drama.

When it comes to natural wonders, nothing beats South Africa's game sanctuaries and the thrill of discovering and photographing lions, rhinos, hippos and buffaloes going about their daily lives. The trophies are often so near that a telephoto lens or binoculars would serve no purpose. And waiting for the big game, you'll develop a new awareness of the trees and flowers, butterflies and birds along the way. Everybody falls under the spell of South Africa's natural kingdom (there are ten major national parks plus many provincial reserves and private game-parks). You don't even have to be the outdoor type...or wild about animals.

For the energetic, the sports

possibilities cover a lot of ground (golf, hiking, horse-riding) and a lot of ocean (swimming, surfing, fishing). Rugby, cricket, boxing and horse-racing draw the big crowds. When it comes to nightlife, South Africa can only, admittedly, make modest claims, but the cities do offer theatres, concerts, cinemas, even nightclubs and discos. The restaurants are noted for gargantuan portions of wholesome food; meals can be accompanied by superb Cape wines, sherries, ports and brandies.

Another useful distraction is shopping, with the emphasis on the work of African artists and artisans. Or you can take home an animal skin (quite legal) or a diamond, or an ostrich egg!

But the longest-lasting souvenir is free: the golden memory of highveld and lowveld and oceans, of cities and hamlets and their easy-going inhabitants, and of the illustrious animals who got here first.

South Africa in a Nutshell

Geography: Africa's southernmost country, the Republic of South Africa, comprises four provinces with an area of 437,877 square miles (some 1,134,000 square kilometres). Most of the country occupies a plateau with an average altitude of 1,200 metres (nearly 4,000 feet). The climate is generally warm and temperate.

Population: At the 1988 census, South Africa counted nearly 30 million inhabitants. According to the ethnic classifications, 17% of the population was white, 10% "coloured" (people of mixed race), 3% Asian and 70% black.

Religion: Most South Africans list themselves as Christians, but there are significant communities of Hindus, Muslims and Jews. Several million blacks adhere to African independent sects, of which some 3,000 have been listed.

Government: Republic with executive State President, three houses of elected representatives elected by white, "coloured" and Indian voters respectively, and an appointed President's Council including non-whites.

Economy: Official emphasis on free enterprise. Noted for exports of gold, uranium, platinum, diamonds, etc.

13

A Brief History

Although the Republic of South Africa (established in 1961) is among the world's younger countries, it can claim to have been inhabited much longer than most.

About 1,800,000 years ago, an ape-man now known by the catchy name of Australopithecus Africanus lived scarcely 20 miles north-west of the site of Johannesburg. So we are told from the radioactive carbon dating of a skull and thigh bone found in the Sterkfontein caves.

The next fateful date on South Africa's prehistoric calendar is a mere 50,000 years ago. That's when a standing, thinking man of the familiar Homo Sapiens family moved into a cave in the eastern Transvaal.

By the 5th century A.D., Bantu-speaking black Africans are believed to have brought an iron-age culture to the Transvaal, the site of thousands of prehistoric mines. Other early inhabitants of the subcontinent were smaller, lighter-skinned people. The white settlers gave the cattle-herders the name of Hottentots and the hunters, Bushmen. Today they are classified as Khokhoi and San and, for general purposes, the composite term is Khoisan.

By the middle of the 17th century, when the first European settlers arrived, several black nations had migrated from the centre of the continent to southern Africa. Notable among them were the Venda, the Sotho-Tswana, the Tsonga and the Nguni. Until the mid-18th century there was no major contact between the white settlers and the blacks; the Khokhoi (Hottentots) began to act as middle-men. But their numbers declined through war and disease, and finally they just faded away, intermarrying with the Europeans and their slaves and blending into what became known as the Cape Coloured population. The surviving San, or Bushmen, retreated to the Kalahari desert, where their descendants still eke out a living.

Dutch Cape

Portuguese explorers had been rounding the Cape of Good Hope (originally called the Cape of Storms) since the end of the 15th century. But in their haste towards the riches of the East, they never got around to founding a colony in South Africa. The British toyed with the idea as early as 1615 when they deposited a handful of

convicts at Table Bay (now Cape Town). But nothing came of it. The unenthusiastic pioneers hitch-hiked back to civilization on a passing ship.

Destiny caught up with South Africa in 1652 when the mighty Dutch East India Company set up a permanent outpost at Table Bay. The company operated trading posts and other holdings from the Caribbean to Formosa and Japan. The modest goal for Table Bay was to provide

Early South African Bushmen are portrayed inside the Cango Caves.

water, food and repair facilities for the company's ships rounding the tip of Africa. The little colony kept its Dutch character even after the arrival of other nationalities, mostly French Huguenot refugees (who added some expertise to the Cape wine industry). The immigrants, dispersed around the countryside, were obliged to learn the Dutch **15**

language. They added a special fervour to the Calvinist tone of the colony's official Dutch Reformed Church. A new people, the Afrikaners or Boers (from the Dutch word, *boer,* farmer), were being forged.

Enter the British

Feuds and wars in Europe sent shock-waves as far as South Africa. In a triangular settling of accounts to avenge the House of Orange for a French attack, the British occupied the Cape colony in 1795. They returned in 1806 and again, definitively, in 1814 as a postscript to the Napoleonic wars.

The effect of this change of management went to the foundations of the Cape society. For instance, the British parliament outlawed the slave trade in 1807 and abolished slavery throughout the empire in 1836. Facing a curtailed labour supply with inadequate compensation, and the subordination of their closely knit culture to English values and language, the hard core of the colonials began planning to strike out on their own into the wilderness. The pioneers became known as the Voortrekkers (literally,

Ideals of Voortrekkers are kept alive in a small Transvaal town.

"those who move to the front") and their odyssey is celebrated wherever Afrikaans is spoken.

Fighting a hostile terrain, marauding tribes and malarial mosquitos, the Boers forced their wagon trains deep into the heart of the subcontinent. A new British colony on the Indian Ocean coast of Natal restricted the Voortrekkers to the interior, where they claimed their own land and the right to pursue their own way of life in two new states: the Orange Free State between the rivers Orange and Vaal, and the Transvaal Republic on the further side of the Vaal River. The clash of interests between British and Boers was to grate quietly until the turn of the century and end in a war of barbaric cruelty.

Meanwhile, fighting between white settlers and black tribesmen had been going on intermittently since the second half of the 18th century. Major frontier wars with the Xhosa, for instance, were fought every ten or 12 years. The struggle for usable land also underlay the wars of black against white, the most dramatic being the blitzkrieg waged by the Zulu general named Shaka. Nation after black nation fled to new homelands before the invincible Zulu hordes.

Glittering Hopes

Nature, which had so far dealt the colonists drought, hungry lions and tsetse flies, proved kinder in the second half of the 19th century.

In the aptly named village of Hopetown, on the Orange River, the first South African diamond was discovered in 1866. When a second stone, of 83.5 carats, turned up, the area was invaded by fortune-hunters. But soon the action shifted about 75 miles to the north: at Kimberley diamonds were found to be as common as seashells on a beach. Over the next 40 years the pursuit of gems created the world's biggest excavation. The Big Hole of Kimberley—a mile around and half as deep—eventually yielded three tons of diamonds (14 ½ million carats).

Gold had been found in various parts of South Africa, but the big strike came in 1886 on the 50-mile-long Transvaal prairie called the Witwatersrand, or Rand for short, destined to become the site of Johannesburg. The prospector was an Australian named George Harrison. He sold his claim for ten pounds and was never heard of again. The reef he found and abandoned has produced more than 35,000 *tons* of pure gold.

Before the gold bonanza, Britain had kept fairly remote from events in the independent Transvaal. But with the Rand's riches unearthed, and foreign prospectors and entrepreneurs flocking in, the idea occurred to "destabilize" the republic's Boer government. Cecil Rhodes, the mining magnate who also served as prime minister of Cape Province, plotted an uprising of the Transvaal's *uitlanders* (foreigners), but it flopped. Three years later, in 1899, the British and the Afrikaners fought it out in the open, once and for all.

The Anglo-Boer War

The Afrikaners were led by the long-time president of the Transvaal, the bearded, top-hatted Paul Kruger. Three of his military chiefs—Louis Botha, Jan Smuts and J.B.M. Hertzog—were destined to become prime ministers of the Union of South Africa. Outnumbered by a ratio of five to one, the Boers held their own through innovative commando tactics.

The British strategist, Lord Kitchener, replied with scorched earth reprisals. During the Anglo-Boer War, as it is called in South Africa, the British also devised the world's first concentration camps. The original intention had been to protect neutral or sympathetic Afrikaners from retaliation at the hands of the Boer commandos, but the idea was soon perverted: the families of Boer soldiers were incarcerated in punitive concentration camps. Some 26,000 inmates died,

Tourists queue to touch gold bar; slag heap, right, shows proximity of mines to central Johannesburg.

mostly of disease. (Much less publicized were the conditions in separate concentration camps the British built for blacks; more than 13,000 died.) The revelations shocked British public opinion and strengthened the inward-looking brotherhood of the Afrikaners.

After two and a half years of fighting, the Boers conceded defeat in May, 1902. What emerged was a British dominion, the Union of South Africa, an amalgam of the conquered Orange Free State and Transvaal with the two British colonies, the Cape and Natal. So delicate were regional sensibilities that the power bases were spread about. This explains why Pretoria is the administrative capital, Bloemfontein the judicial capital, and Cape Town the seat of parliament. Foreshadowing future racial policies, it was decided at this early stage that membership in the national parliament would be for whites only.

The World Wars and Aftermath

Only four years after creating the Union of South Africa, Britain was at war with imperial Germany in the "war to end all wars". South African troops were assigned to the conquest of German territories in east and west Africa. Joining the mainstream, a South African brigade was sent to fight alongside the Allies in Egypt, then France and Belgium; it suffered grave casualties and surrendered.

By the time World War II broke out, General Smuts was in his second term as prime minister. Overcoming a powerful minority in parliament in favour of neutrality, he led South Africa into the war against Nazi Germany. South African troops fought in North Africa and Italy; about 9,000 died.

General Smuts, one of the founders of the United Nations in 1945, drafted the human rights declaration of the organization's charter. But South Africa was almost immediately under fire for its own human rights record. Resolutions condemning South African racial policies soon became routine, and the country pulled out of Unesco, the World Health Organization and other agencies.

Under pressure from within the multi-racial Commonwealth, South Africa withdrew from its historic relationship with Britain, becoming an independent republic in 1961. Its isolation was intensified in 1962 when the UN General Assembly called on all member states to cut diplomatic relations with South Africa. (Western nations rejected this advice.)

Society Under Tension

The policies which so dramatically changed the image of South Africa from a defender of democracy in World War II to an international pariah were summed up by the Afrikaans word *apartheid*. It became an internationally understood word after the election of the first all-Afrikaner government in South Africa in 1948. The web of laws for racial separation and control was spun by Dr. Hendrik Verwoerd, Minister of Native Affairs and later Prime Minister. He was assassinated in 1966, but his programme continued to gain strength.

Violent protests against apartheid, and the government's reaction to the unrest, have kept South Africa under the international spotlight. Objections to the pass laws, affecting all blacks, culminated in a demonstration at Sharpeville, in the Transvaal. There, in 1960, the police opened fire on the crowd, killing 69 blacks and wounding 178. The world was stunned. In Soweto in 1976, more than a week of violence brought 176 deaths and more than a thousand injuries.

The government banned individuals and organizations suspected of subversion. Alleged trouble-makers were held without charge or trial; dozens died in custody.

New unrest sweeping the townships in the middle of the 1980s prompted the government to declare a state of emergency. Thousands of people, nearly all of them black, were arrested and held without trial. Violence dominated TV screens abroad until news crews were barred from the scene.

Amid heightening internal and external pressures for change, the government scrapped some crucial aspects of apartheid. Then in 1990 the ANC and other banned organizations were legalized and the foremost black leader, Nelson Mandela, was released after 27 years in prison. Despite growing tensions between conservatives and reformers, the world watched with hope as a critical new era unfolded.

Where to Go

South Africa sprawls over an area bigger than West Germany, Holland, Belgium, France and Italy combined —clearly too big a country to get to know in a single visit. This book makes no attempt at listing all the republic's attractions, concentrating instead on the areas covered by most package tours and individual foreign tourists. The South African tourist authorities define these areas as Bushveld Transvaal, Leisureland Natal and Coastal Cape.

We begin the highlights with Johannesburg, the biggest and liveliest city in the republic, sprawling out over a plateau a mile above sea level. After a look at the nearby capital of Pretoria, we head east from highveld to low for a survey of South Africa's prime tourist attraction, the Kruger National Park. After a quick change of pace at a hedonistic outpost called Sun City, we head over the mountains to the Indian Ocean. Leaving busy Durban and its beaches we follow the coast clockwise through the Garden Route area to the Cape of Good Hope.

Focusing on a cross-section of the beauties and excitements of South Africa, this itinerary **21** necessarily crowds out huge chunks of the rest of the country. Virtually the whole Orange Free State is omitted, and a man-made marvel of the calibre of Kimberley's Big Hole has had to be overlooked (it would entail hundreds of miles of extra travel). For cruel reasons of limited space, the Kalahari Gemsbok Park and other important game preserves have not been included. These and other sights merit leisurely exploration—a good reason for a return trip to South Africa.

Johannesburg

Most of the world's great cities were built alongside rivers, but Johannesburg had to make do with an underground stream. Of gold! That was enough to transform it in three years from meagre grazing land to the biggest town in South Africa. A century later, it's a dynamic metropolis of a bit more than two million people.

You can tell that gold made this city: streets have names like Claim and Nugget, and even if you didn't notice the superstructures, a bit like oil derricks, over the old mine shafts, you couldn't miss the man-made hills. If these were beaches, their colour would be a dream, but as cityscape they're like transplants from outer space. Not much can be done to beautify slag heaps, though they've found heroic species of grass and bush that can survive in the cyanide-soaked soil. (The wild and woolly mining atmosphere has been re-created in Gold Reef City, a recent development south-east of Johannesburg.)

The boom-town pace hasn't entirely given way to late 20th-century sophistication and success. The pedestrians still bustle about as if they were hurrying to stake a claim. Some attribute this animation to the altitude—nearly 1,750 metres (more than 5,700 feet). But don't count on the thinner air making you more energetic than usual; some visitors tire easily at this altitude.

Johannesburg is at its best in summer (from around November to March). Warm sunny mornings may turn into thundery afternoons, but the torrential rains soon move on, leaving the city refreshed and the countryside green. In winter, however, the dry winds are cold and the grass goes brown.

Like all South African cities, Johannesburg's historic population patterns have been dislocated by the racial separation

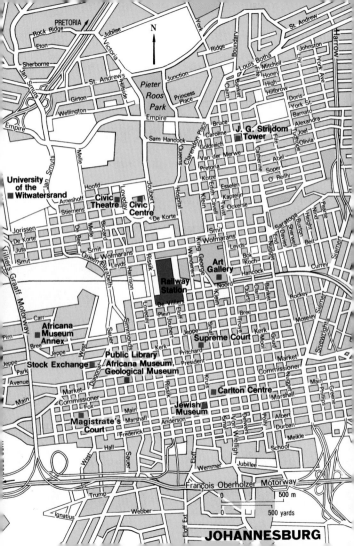

JOHANNESBURG

laws. Thus some 50,000 Asians were resettled in their own suburb, Lenasia, and the blacks are assigned to vast townships on the outskirts; Soweto, by far the biggest and best known, is home for perhaps two million people.

For a fast survey of the city, from Soweto to the smart northern suburbs, with the central skyscrapers in the foreground, an excellent vantage point is the top of the 50-storey Carlton Centre. From the observation floor (admission is charged) you can follow the trail of the gold seam east, south and west of the heart of the city; the eruptions of sand-coloured dross mountains reveal the path of the reef.

The Carlton complex (Africa's biggest commercial structure) includes a 600-room hotel in a skyscraper which bottoms

Discreet skyscrapers tower over mile-high heart of Johannesburg.

out as a pyramid, a huge shopping centre, and a parking garage for 2,000 cars. On the 46th floor, a municipal tourist information office offers free maps, leaflets and hotel reservations.

With all the new office buildings in town it's hard to find any historical monuments (in Johannesburg this means anything before World War I). But local preservationists are proud of the **Rissik Street Post Office,** begun in 1897. After the Anglo-Boer War, the British modified the red-brick building, adding an extra floor and a clock tower. The afterthoughts come off well.

The **Johannesburg Public Library,** on a small park behind the colonnaded City Hall, is the country's biggest, housing 700,000 volumes. Upstairs is the **Africana Museum,** specializing in the history of the early settlers of South Africa. There is a good collection of Cape silver and sturdy old pioneer furniture, and a 19th-century stagecoach. A Victorian pub has been reconstructed, as well as an old-fashioned pharmacy with ceramic drug jars from as early as the 17th century.

The library's Africana Museum now covers only the history of the white population of the country, with a separate section on early Johannesburg. Exhibits on black African history and culture have been moved to a new, much larger **annex** in the former Newtown fruit and vegetable market in Bree Street. Under the lofty ceiling, full-sized models of tribal huts have been laid out in typical village patterns. On display are utensils, jewellery, weapons, musical instruments and costumes. There are stone-age paintings of animals and hunters, often depicted with astonishing skill and sophistication.

West of the Newtown market is a big modern shopping centre called **Oriental Plaza.** The smell of spices greets you even before you arrive. A delightful peacock statue-fountain adorns a patio surrounded by Indian restaurants, snack bars, and hundreds of shops selling Indian trinkets and bargain-priced western fashions. If you can't make it to Durban, where Indians make up the majority of the population, this sample of eastern atmosphere is worth a visit.

Back among the skyscrapers, **Diagonal Street** is short but important. When you see a newspaper headline reporting that Diagonal Street is buoyant or bored or even gravely ill, it's only a figure of speech. Diagonal Street, like New York's Wall Street, symbolizes the stock exchange of the same address. The new Johannesburg **Stock Exchange** building, at Diagonal and Pritchard Streets, may be visited Monday to Friday; free guided tours include an effective audiovisual show on the riches of South Africa and a look at the brokers in action on the floor.

The Johannesburg railway station, Africa's largest, was built in the 1960s in a style reminiscent of Mussolini's Termini in Rome. Before the introduction of reforms by the South African government, non-whites used a separate part of the building and rode in separate carriages. Every day some 200,000 blacks commute between Johannesburg and Soweto.

In the old south building of the station a small **railway museum** is packed with memorabilia of transport in South Africa: a real 1890 locomotive, model trains, planes and ships, and the kind of gadgets and details that fascinate collectors. There are actual platform-ticket machines, lanterns, ticket-punchers, dining car place-settings, and switching control panels.

The **Johannesburg Art Gallery** (closed on Mondays) is nicely situated in Joubert Park, the city's oldest park, east of the railway station. The building was designed by Sir Edwin Lutyens, the esteemed British architect. The collection starts with El Greco and 17th-century Dutch painters but devotes most of its space to the 19th and early 20th centuries. A small but representative display of South African art brings the show up to date.

Johannesburg's most popular museum is the **South African National Museum of Military History** (formerly called the War Museum) in Hermanus Ekstein Park in the northern suburb of Saxonwold. Aside from the expectable battle flags, uniforms and medals, plenty of military hardware is on show, from oldtime flintlocks to World War II tanks.

An unusual **monument** stands at the top of Rissik Street, a few blocks north of the railway station. The Chamber of Mines donated it, in honour of the gold miners. It is composed of the statues of three miners—two black and

A study in black and white: chess under the Carlton Centre's dome.

one white—at work with a big pneumatic drill.

Beyond is the new **Civic Centre**, with a novel triangular floor plan to contain a hive of municipal activity, the local bureaucracy having long since outgrown the original City Hall. Alongside, the modern Civic Theatre provides seasons of drama, opera and ballet. A modern fountain features statues of three happy dancers at play.

Westwards lie the campuses of Johannesburg's two universities. The University of the Witwatersrand ("Wits" for short—pronounced Vits) is Africa's biggest English-language university. A historic relic in front of the university library is the original **cross** which the Portuguese explorer Bartholomew Dias erected near Port Elizabeth in 1488. To the west of "Wits" is South Africa's most modern campus; at the new Rand Afrikaans University, classes are conducted in Afrikaans.

Called the tallest structure in all Africa, the **J.G. Strijdom Tower** is a communications relay post 269 metres (883 feet) high. The design, drably functional, included an observation deck, now closed for security reasons. The tower blindly overhangs the neigh-

All races converge in a shopping street; above: a part of Soweto.

bourhood called **Hillbrow**, a cosmopolitan district with a relatively animated nightlife—a great deal more, in any event, than you'll find along the sepulchral streets of the central business district after the throngs have gone home to the suburbs. (Johannesburg's other, more ornamental, tower, in Brixton, belongs to the South African Broadcasting Corporation.)

As bizarre an excursion as you'll ever experience is a sightseeing tour of **Soweto**. The West Rand Administration Board, which controls the affairs of black Africans here, runs bus tours on Monday to Friday mornings; private tour companies also schedule Soweto trips. The names of the visitors must be registered with the Administration Board.

"Soweto" sounds as African as "Lesotho" or "Basuto", but that's coincidental. It's a contraction of "South Western Townships". Here approximately a million blacks live in what the authorities describe as 29 "quaint, neat box-like houses" as well as "imposing mansions". It's all rather like visiting a safari park, being driven through endless residential streets, staring out of the bus at the inhabitants as they wait for buses or hang out the washing. There are stops, though, at a model kindergarten, a folklore park and a modern shopping centre run by blacks. Other bright spots to contrast with most of the township's neighbourhoods are the new subdivisions of middle-class black housing and the exclusive streets called Millionaires' Row. Though it's anything but a merry way to spend a morning, the Soweto excursion is a worthwhile undertaking for anyone trying to understand the problems of South Africa.

Another educational excursion—much more popular—involves a trip through a real **gold mine**. Anyone but a professional miner will get a thrill out of this one—going down to a shaft 220 metres (722 feet) below ground decked out in boots, yellow raincoats, protective hats and miners' lamps. Even children are allowed to go along, though some of the younger ones are unsettled by the claustrophobia and darkness of half an hour below the surface, and by the loud noise of demonstration drillings.

The **Gold Mine Museum** was established by the South African Chamber of Mines at the site of 14 Shaft of Crown Mines, in Alamein Road. The discovery and exploitation of gold is well illustrated, and then the visitors are shown around a replica of a miners' village and a working model of a gold processing system. Visitors see molten gold poured into a mould to form a 25-kilogramme ingot. After it cools, the tourists line up to get their hands on the bar, worth about a quarter of a million dollars—to pick it up but not to take it home, the guide explains.

South Africa's gold mines employ about a quarter of a million underground workers, mostly black contract labourers recruited in neighbouring countries.

Every Sunday, miners from one or another region put on skins and feathers and perform **tribal dances** for the tourists in an amphitheatre on the grounds of the Gold Mine Museum. Tour companies run excursions or, if you have a car, you can go unescorted at a considerable saving.

Supplementing the facilities of the museum and the historic

14 Shaft, the Chamber of Mines arranges visits to working gold mines elsewhere in the area. Children under 16 are not allowed to go along. Various tour operators offer Sunday excursions including the mine workers' tribal dancing at the museum.

Pretoria

The best time to visit pretty Pretoria is in the southern hemisphere's spring—October and November. That's the season when the city's 60,000 jacaranda trees burst into colour, a spectacle of delicate beauty. The trees are not indigenous; they were imported from Brazil. Even if the petals have been swept away by the time you arrive, you'll find Pretoria an uncommonly agreable city with beautiful parks and innovative architecture.

Pretoria's metropolitan area has a population of about 750,000. Unlike other major cities in South Africa, Pretoria has a majority of whites, many working in government jobs, for this is the administrative capital of the republic as well as the provincial capital of the Transvaal.

The historic heart of Pretoria is **Church Square**, where the early settlers built their first church in the 1850s. In the middle of the square stands a statue of Paul Kruger, a rugged pioneer who was elected President four times in the late 19th century. Around the base of the monument are statues of four rifle-toting citizen-soldiers of the era. Photographers with instant cameras stake out this spot, waiting for backwoods tourists who need proof that they visited the capital.

Facing the square are some distinguished official buildings of earlier days: the old **Raadsaal** (parliament) in Italian Renaissance style, the **South African Reserve Bank,** designed by the famous architect Sir Herbert Baker, and the **Palace of Justice,** used as a hospital during the British occupation of 1900.

Near the square some adventurous modern buildings have raised the skyline and planted futuristic shopping centres. The **Volkskas-sentrum,** new headquarters of the first Afrikaner-controlled bank, has observation areas on the 37th floor, reached by a "wall climber lift". The slow ride up the outside wall of the building puts into dramatic perspective the city's situation on a plateau protected by a circle of distant hills. **31**

Strijdom Square, just down the street from the Volkskas skyscraper, honours J.G. Strijdom, prime minister in the 1950s, with a bust about 50 times life-size—the sort of sculpture one would expect to find in Moscow or Bucharest. Softening the effect is a dynamic statue of four bronze horses above a fountain. Beyond the square, in the plaza between the new state opera and theatre, a happy modern semi-abstract statue called *Applause* revolves on its base.

The theatre complex, comprising four auditoriums, may be viewed on guided tours (see p. 120).

Planners of Pretoria's huge new municipal office building neatly sidestepped the issue of whether to give it an Afrikaans or an English name; they called it Munitoria. This standard modern office building, bigger than most, is of interest to tourists because it contains the Visitors Information Bureau, offering local maps, leaflets and advice.

Afrikaner pioneers remembered: Voortrekker Monument, Pretoria.

If you can't manage a trip to a game park—a gross misfortune for any visitor to South Africa—you might want to look in at Pretoria's **National Zoological Gardens.** Some 3,500 species are said to reside here, amidst showy flower gardens; for a different point of view, a cable-car floats above some areas. But however you look at it, the difference between a zoo and a natural game preserve is the difference between a greenhouse and a rain forest.

Next door to the zoo, the **National Cultural History and Open Air Museum** has a bit of something for everyone, from stone age rock engravings to an exact replica of General Smuts' bedroom. There are old wagons and cannon and a room full of historic bibles, including one pierced by a bomb splinter in the Anglo-Boer War. The hoard of silver bowls, pots and pitchers from the Cape Colony of the 18th century is called the best in the nation.

Sir Herbert Baker designed Pretoria's most noble architectural ensemble, the **Union Buildings,** a couple of mirror-image buildings linked by a semi-circular colonnade. This big ministerial complex looks down on simply gorgeous formal terraced gardens of brilliant flowers, sculpted trees and lawns worthy of golf-green status. The basement of the Union Buildings contains the South African State Archives.

Bird-watchers don't know which way to turn in South Africa, where even suburban gardens harbour the most exotic birds—locally based songsters and transients in wild colour schemes. For a rapid initiation course, swoop in on the **Transvaal Museum** in Paul Kruger Street, where every species of South African bird is identified. Among other educational devices there is a sort of juke-box for bird calls. The museum, a national research organization, also deals in butterflies, reptiles, prehistoric bones and other aspects of natural history.

South of Pretoria, in the Fountains Valley Nature Reserve, a military stronghold built in 1898 commands strategic views of Pretoria and the fertile countryside. **Fort Klapperkop's** history is rather short on drama: it missed action in the Anglo-Boer War and served as an ammunition dump during World War II. Today the fort is spruced up as a museum of the military history of the "Zuid-Afrikaansche Republiek", the Transvaal republic of the Boers.

Bright new buildings raise sky-line of gardened capital, Pretoria.

For miles around Pretoria you can see the **Voortrekker Monument** on its hilltop. From afar it might be mistaken for an electric power station or some such windowless leviathan. But its purpose is purely symbolic—a shrine dedicated to the fortitude of the pioneers of the 1830s who trekked from the Cape to the Transvaal to perpetuate their religion, language and austere way of life.

Inside the granite monument, an aperture in the high domed roof is placed so that at noon every December 16th a beam of sunlight penetrates to a crypt far below, illuminating the inscription on a sarcophagus: *Ons vir jou, Suid-Afrika* (meaning "We're for You, South Africa"). December 16th is the anniversary of the 1838 Battle of Blood River. Avenging the murder of the Voortrekker leader Piet Retief and 70 of his men, the Boers killed about 3,000 Zulu warriors, at a cost of only four whites wounded. (For visiting hours, see p. 120.)

Down the hill is a **museum** containing the Voortrekker Tapestry. This series of needle-work panels depicting events of the Great Trek occupied nine patriotic women for eight years. The museum also has dioramas illustrating pioneer life; the typical Boer living room might be mistaken for an old Dutch farm scene… except for the lion skin on the floor!

Forty kilometres east of Pretoria, at **Cullinan,** is the Premier Diamond Mine, a historic site in its own right. The diamond to beat all diamonds—3,106 carats—was un-

earthed here in 1905. From the fist-sized stone was hewn the Star of Africa and other gems now listed among the British Crown Jewels. The mine is still in business, producing about a million carats a year, though most of the stones go for industrial purposes. Tour operators in Johannesburg and Pretoria run excursions to the mine, or by car. Tours of the workings are scheduled eight times a week; wear heavy shoes (for hours, see p. 120).

Eastern Transvaal

The name Transvaal means the "land across the Vaal", the river dividing two provinces, the Transvaal and the Orange Free State. The Vaal River (its name means "grey" in Afrikaans) irrigates thousands of square miles of farms, and provides the water Pretoria and the Witwatersrand drinks.

From Pretoria or Johannesburg to the Kruger National Park (see pp. 39–49) is about **35**

400 kilometres, much of it on excellent roads, including dual carriageways separated by parkland. The trip eastwards starts out through the grassy plains of the highveld; less than half-way to Kruger Park, the scenery undergoes sensational changes. One minute you think you could be in Scotland, the next the hills are as rugged as North Dakota. And suddenly the winding road plunges from cool spruce forests to banana plantations on the hot, humid lowveld.

If you're in a rush, you can fly to the Kruger Park. Less hurried travellers drive, or take coach tours, going out and back efficiently on Route N 4. If you have a day or two to spare, however, it's infinitely more interesting to take one route to Kruger, leave the park through another gate, and return to the Rand by a different road.

Here are some of the places to look out for in the eastern Transvaal:

Nelspruit. The river here is called the Crocodile, and that's not the only tropical touch. This is the citrus belt. The town is surrounded by orange groves, as well as farms producing fruits like mangoes, lichees and avocados. Nelspruit itself is a handsome regional

centre of more than 15,000 people, with parks, sports facilities and original buildings.

Pilgrim's Rest. Amidst delightful pastoral scenery, this looks like a film-set version of an old gold-mining town. But it's real. A prospector named Alec "Wheelbarrow" Patterson first panned gold here in 1873. Inevitably, news of the easy pickings soon spread, and Pilgrim's Rest took on all the trappings of a gold-rush town; 18 pubs could hardly cope with the crowds of carousing miners. In the 20th century mining technology became more sophisticated, and the gold effectively ran out in 1972. When the mining operations were shut down, the provincial authorities bought up what would have become a ghost town and preserved it as an oasis of nostalgia. There are museums, gold-panning demonstrations, souvenir shops with fresh ideas, and charming hotels.

Blyde River Canyon. "Awe-inspiring" is no exaggeration for the views in this part of the world, where the Drakensberg mountains herald the transition from highveld to low.

Gold rush era relics in museum at Pilgrim's Rest; Bourke's Luck gorge recalls one man's bonanza.

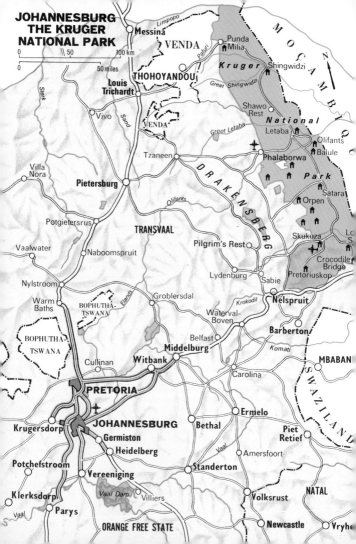

The geological surprises of the escarpment include rock-faces of cliffs weirdly coloured by lichens and algae.

The gorge itself looks like some awful mistake committed by nature—where everything turned out beautifully in the end. Three sandstone peaks —round outcroppings topped with grass-covered cupolas— are called the **Three Rondavels.** Beyond is the hulking **Mariepskop,** a mountain squared off like an aircraft carrier. Hillsides plunge to the river zigzagging through the creases, widening at last behind the new Blyde River Dam.

From **God's Window,** a divine panorama of lowveld is revealed. Near Bourke's Luck, named after an old gold mine, the rivers Blyde ("joyful") and Treur ("sorrowful") converge in a three-way gorge. Three aluminium bridges offer staggering views of this natural drama, from thundering waterfalls to pot-holes that seem to have been excavated by some gigantic ice-cream scoop.

An unexpected island of luxury in the area is the **Blydepoort Public Resort,** a large state-run holiday village laid out like a prosperous suburb, with air-conditioned chalets, restaurants, gardens and many sports facilities.

Kruger Park

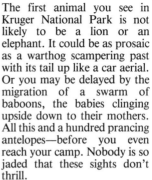

The first animal you see in Kruger National Park is not likely to be a lion or an elephant. It could be as prosaic as a warthog scampering past with its tail up like a car aerial. Or you may be delayed by the migration of a swarm of baboons, the babies clinging upside down to their mothers. All this and a hundred prancing antelopes—before you even reach your camp. Nobody is so jaded that these sights don't thrill.

If you equate a safari with roughing it, you've come to the wrong place. The "huts" have air-conditioning, the supermarket is stocked to the ceiling, the bank and post office are right in the park, and a five-course dinner is served on white linen tablecloths. It's all comfortable enough to attract little old ladies, wheelchair adventurers, and families with barefoot infants—all enjoying the holiday of their lives.

Kruger National Park, about the size of Massachusetts, is South Africa's biggest wildlife sanctuary. It contains more species than any other game reserve on the continent of Africa. Among the animals everyone wants to see, the 1980 census counted about 7,500 elephants, 27,000 buffalo, 22,000 zebra and 120,000 impala. On the other side of the ledger, close to 400,000 humans are clocked in every year.

Accommodation in the parks may be reserved one year in advance. You can book through a travel agency or direct by writing to the National Parks Board, P.O. Box 787, Pretoria 0001. If you wait until the last minute, you still stand a chance if you telephone the reservation service at (012) 343-1991, or fax (343-0905). The complexities are all computerized, so you'll have your answer in a matter of seconds.

If no space is available, you might consider joining one of the package tours; the operators make block bookings in Kruger Park. Or you can try to find accommodation in a hotel or camping ground outside the park but near enough for you to go in as a day-tripper.

The range of accommodation inside the park should please all kinds of visitors, from the campers to the pampered. Simpler housing runs to thatched huts with or without showers and toilets. At the top of the scale are family cottages with kitchenettes and bathrooms with hot and cold running water. Many are air-conditioned—a relief in a territory where the mercury has been known to hit 47° C (116° F). But the average daily maximum temperature in mid-summer is a relatively comfortable 30° C (86° F).

Warts and all: muddy pool is scene of warthog family reunion.

Predicting the weather for Kruger National Park is risky. Among other things, it's more than 300 kilometres from top to bottom. The south gets three times as much rain as the north-east of the park. The rainy season extends from September or October to March or April—mostly fast thunder-showers, not the sort of rain that will significantly affect your plans.

One bit of shopping which won't wait until you arrive in the park: a medical imperative. Kruger Park and the private reserves alongside it are in a malaria zone. Ask your pharmacist or doctor to explain the pre-

cautions you must take. Or you can go to any pharmacy in South Africa and buy anti-malaria pills over the counter. Normally you must start taking the pills several days before entering the affected district and continue the specified dosage for several weeks after leaving. A syrup is made for children.

The Camps

There are 14 rest camps, mostly in the southern half of the park. (Most tourists arrive by gates in the south.) Among the biggest and best equipped camps, from south to north:

Lower Sabie. Very near the eastern edge of the park (the Mozambique border), Lower Sabie is also a short ride from the southern extremity of the park—the Crocodile River. Crocodiles and hippos are the obvious river denizens to look for, but buffalo are important, too.

Pretoriuskop. This large, old camp enjoys the park's only swimming pool (the authorities think any more swimming might disturb the environment). Look for lions, giraffe and zebra in this area.

Skukuza. More beds than any other camp, and more facilities, including a library of more than 5,000 books about wildlife in English, Afrikaans, French and German. Lions, giraffe and elephants are familiar sights hereabouts.

Satara. A large, well-planned camp with huts in a big circle around a pretty lawn and flower garden. Elephants come to gambol at nearby dams.

Olifants. As the name indicates, this is elephant country. The camp enjoys a majestic hilltop setting commanding the hippopotamus-haunted Olifants River.

Letaba. Near the Phalaborwa Gate, on a steep hill overlooking the wide Letaba River. You might roll out of bed here to see a couple of elephants munching the grass down below. Lions and hyenas provide the nocturnal sound-effects.

All camps in the park have accommodation for white visitors, but only four of them accept tourists of other races (in separate sections): Lower Sabie, Skukuza, Satara and Letaba.

Cast of Characters

All the creatures in the park, from the dowdy rhinoceros to the elegant impala, have something profound to tell us about nature and life. Here is a sampler of a dozen leading characters in Kruger's all-star cast...in alphabetical order.

Antelope. This is a generic term for animals as diverse as the gazelle and the wildebeest. All antelope ruminate (chew cud). All males and some females have horns, some in dramatic shapes and sizes but never in the form of antlers. Of the 19 species of antelope at large in the park, the overwhelming majority are impala. With their two-toned coats and (males only) symmetrically curved horns, impala are as pretty as you'll find— and acrobatic. Watch them fly through the air, leaping twice their height with ease. (One antelope you *won't* see is the springbok, South Africa's national symbol, which is concentrated in the Kalahari region.)

Baboon. The dog-faced chacma baboon has a worried look, perhaps wondering whether any of the tourists will offer a handout. (Don't! It's bad for their diet and personality, and they could hurt you.) A troop of baboons is full of individualists, held in line by the big, dominant males, who grow to weigh nearly 90 pounds. They can live to 45...unless a leopard gets there first.

Buffalo. In spite of the menacing size and shape of its heavy horns, the Cape buffalo *looks* peaceful enough—yet it can put up a fierce struggle with a lion. Since buffalo are steady drinkers, they like to stay close to waterholes or rivers. Buffalo are more active at night, though, preferring to play it cool when the hot sun shines.

Cheetah. You can recognize this sleek cat by the distinct marks running down from its eyes to the corners of the mouth, as if worn away by tears. The cheetah is different in other ways: it purrs but can't roar; its claws can't be fully sheathed; and it hunts in broad daylight. Called the fastest of animals, the cheetah has been clocked at more than 60 miles per hour over short distances— which is the secret of its success.

Elephant. While the cheetah is relatively rare in Kruger Park (only about 300 at last count), the elephant population (about 7,500) grows so rapidly that several hundred are doomed to be culled every year. The problem is ecological: they eat and drink too much, stripping forests and slurping waterholes dry. Other than that, the African elephant is admirable, especially the loving mothers and their calves. If your car should be surrounded by meandering pachyderms, turn off the engine, keep silent, and wait for the herd to move along.

Giraffe. The stately walking skyscraper is not so easy to see or photograph as you'd think, since its blotchy complexion blends in with the trees. It always seems to be munching leaves, which is why so many trees in Kruger Park are trimmed into unlikely shapes. Giraffes are vulnerable to attack by lions, one good reason they are reluctant to lie down; they sleep standing up, briefly.

Hippopotamus. The piggy eyes and ears of the mighty hippo are what you're most likely to see, protruding from the surface of a river like the periscope of a submarine. Hippos are so ungainly that they're more comfortable afloat than on land. They also gravitate to water because they can't stand the heat. Baby hippos are born under water. A grown-up can stay fully submerged for five minutes, returning to the surface with a spray like a whale.

Hyena. As ridiculous as the hippopotamus looks and acts, it's considerably more appealing than the hyena, skulking about with its should-

Alert to danger, impala keep together; lone baboon on all fours; lion pausing to take a drink.

South African Tourist Board

ers hunched and a face seemingly wrinkled by a guilty conscience. The pro-hyena lobby points out that the alleged scavenger is actually a predator most of the time; nobody criticizes lions for killing to eat, so why pick on the hyena? As for that infamous laugh, or wail, it's all part of the heinous hyena's image problem.

Leopard. Being a nocturnal, lone-wolf sort of hunter, the leopard is hard to find, so any sighting is a big thrill. The best places to look are along rivers, among rocky outcrops, behind foliage or—cats will be cats —up a tree. The leopard is bright and strong enough to haul its kill high into the branches of a tree, where most competitors can't reach it, there to dine at leisure.

Lion. Safari photographers can barely contain that heady feeling at first sight of lions, but snapping a respectable picture is quite a problem. Chances are the animals have dozed off, lying blended into the bush. Or they may be engaged in nothing more blood-curdling than snuggling and playing together. Lionesses, outnumbering the maned males, do most of the hunting, but a hungry male will unchivalrously drive off all the others of the group when it's feeding time.

Rhinoceros. A rhino's front horn can be as long as a trombone with the slide fully extended. Because powdered rhino horn is considered a miraculous aphrodisiac in Asia and parts of Africa, priced higher per ounce than gold, poaching all but wiped out the South African herds. Hundreds have been introduced into Kruger Park. There are two species of rhinoceros, "white" and "black", though they both look the same muddy colour after a good wallow. The so-called black, discernable by its pointed mouth, is the more erratic and aggressive.

Zebra. A common but no less wondrous sight in Kruger Park is a grazing herd of zebra, like toy horses in striped pyjamas. There are close to 20,000 of them in the park, so you'll probably have a good chance to ponder the unsolved problem: why such stunning camouflage? The zebra feeds on grass alone, involving a great deal of migration in search of new fields. High-strung and timid, the herd is likely to bolt at the first hint of danger.

And the **birds.** In your travels through the park, you'll be astonished at the variety of birds that cross your path. Even non-bird-watchers show childish excitement at sight of their first long-tailed shrike or yellow-billed hornbill. You'll also admire guinea fowl, bustards, and the secretary bird —so named for the long feathers hanging from the back of its head like quill pens. Less admired is the vulture, a far-sighted scavenger; if you see them gliding about expectantly, they could be announcing a kill.

Striking a lovable pose, zebra stand guard in typical bushveld scenery, ever on the lookout for lions and other perils at large in Kruger Park.

On the Lookout

Unless you pay attention you could spend hours roaming the park and see nothing wilder than antelope. But driving at an appropriate speed and staying vigilant, you should spot ten or more species in a day.

The best speed is under 25 kilometres per hour. Like a military scout, keep your eyes shifting from near to far, but mainly in the middle distance, alert for any movement or discrepancy. Peer into the shadows, for that's where many animals hide out when it's hot. Pay special attention to water-holes, dams and rivers, where the largest concentrations of animals are seen.

In the African summer the best times for spotting game are from dawn to perhaps 11 a.m. and again in late afternoon. But when the sun is high in the sky

Giraffe stands fast as clients of private game park get a closeup.

it's a mercy to stay in the cool—lunching, reading, bird-watching or having a siesta. The problem is less acute in the cooler season, when the waterholes are active from perhaps 8 a.m. to noon and game can be seen at any time of day.

Wilderness Trails

Perhaps the irony has struck you: in a zoo the animals are caged, but in Kruger Park it's the humans who are confined —to camps and cars. The only way to escape this restriction is to join a Wilderness Trail group —eight hardy people accompanied by an armed tracker and ranger. The trail-followers, travelling by foot, stay out in the bush for three nights. Only a small number of visitors (aged 12 to 60) can be accommodated in this way. Reservations are opened one year in advance, but you may try for a last-minute cancellation.

Private Game Parks

An alternative expedient for getting closer to nature—more comfortable but more expensive—is checking in at a private game park. About half a dozen of these establishments operate in the bushveld alongside the western border of Kruger Park. Two- or three-day package tours are offered, including

scheduled flights from Johannesburg to the air strips at Phalaborwa or Skukuza.

Here are some of the things you can do at a private preserve which are impossible under the Kruger Park regulations: you travel in an open Land-Rover with a ranger and tracker as your guides. You leave the road and drive across the bush if necessary. Radio coordination among the vehicles spreads the word if rare animals are spotted. And night safaris with spotlights bring into focus the nocturnal creatures you might never see at Kruger.

The most luxurious of the private game parks, called Mala Mala, bases its philosophy on "getting away from it all"—comfortably—and you do. The much less expensive Sabi Sabi Game Reserve boasts of its haute cuisine and amiable rangers. Like Mala Mala and Sabi Sabi, several other private establishments have air-conditioned accommodation and swimming pools: Motswari, Inyati and Thornybush Game Lodges. Information, including prices, on these and other commercial game parks, as well as the national parks, is contained in the annual brochure *South Africa Travel Digest,* issued by Satour, the South African Tourism Board.

An African Spree: Sun City

Night people frustrated by early-to-bed Kruger Park, or the austere restrictions of the rest of South Africa, have a handy escape valve in Sun City. This bushveld Las Vegas, within easy day-trip distance of Johannesburg and Pretoria, even offers a suggestion of international adventure.

Sun City has been created under the blue-and-orange flag of the Republic of Bophuthatswana. Opponents of Pretoria's policy of separate development say the so-called independent homelands are a ploy to dispose of significant numbers of South African blacks, and that the republics are mere satellites of South Africa. But in one field at least—that of morality—Bophuthatswana flaunts its independence. Here South Africans can gamble, watch naughty shows, and engage in inter-racial "togetherness" instead of apartheid. If this is all too shocking, outdoor escape may be found on an 18-hole golf-course, an artificial lake for waterskiing and para-sailing, and a game reserve.

If you've never been to Las Vegas, the gambling scene at Sun City's hotel and entertainment complex will dazzle you: some 700 slot machines in mirrored halls so dark you can hardly read your watch. But, then, there's no need to know the time; jackpots (up to 60,000 to one) are disgorged 24 hours a day—though not on Sunday mornings. In the adjoining casino, lissome English girls in long dresses work as croupiers, distracting some of the less hardened gamblers. Thirty-six roulette tables and over 20 blackjack stands cater to most

of the punters, but there are also facilities for American craps, chemmy and punto banco.

Up to 25,000 tourists a day come to Sun City by car, package-tour bus, or air, to take in the glamour of all-star shows, the uninhibited discos, the day and night showings of soft porn films. Children are looked after with games and sports. Souvenir shops sell the handicrafts of the Tswana people and other African gifts, and the post office appeals to collectors with its unusual Bophuthatswana postage stamps. There are no border complications. The frontier dividing South Africa from Bophuthatswana is marked with a casual roadside sign; no formalities, not even a stop sign.

Surrounded by South Africa but free of its taboos, Sun City can offer escapism on various levels.

Natal

The smallest of South Africa's four provinces, Natal, occupies only eight per cent of the nation's territory. But therein lies a huge diversity of geography from snow-prone mountains to nicely baked Indian Ocean beaches. The people, too, range from Anglo to Zulu.

A holiday discovery gave the coast, and eventually the whole province, its name. Vasco da Gama, the Portuguese navigator, first sighted these shores on Christmas Day in 1497. "Natal" is Portuguese for "Christmas".

The Natal Parks Board, established in 1947, has elbowed out the national authorities and controls about 50 provincial parks, reserves and "public resorts" on its own. The policy is to keep the reserves as unspoiled as possible, yet the accommodation can be as comfortable as fully equipped chalets and bungalows. (All the cottages, chalets and camp grounds are now assigned to multi-racial use, with whites-only restrictions no longer in force.)

Several of Natal's most impressive reserves are arrayed among the **Drakensberg mountains** as they delineate the frontier between the province and the Kingdom of Lesotho. Stone-age Bushmen were attracted to these mountains because of the availability of small game to hunt and delicious water to drink. They were driven out by a succession of tribes, most recently the Ngwaneni. It's the Ngwaneni who live within sight of the Drakensberg peaks today, in their traditional "beehive" huts of wattle, shaped like haystacks.

A stupendous geological phenomenon, the **Drakensberg Amphitheatre**, climaxes **Royal Natal National Park**. The panorama looks as if Mount Rushmore had been placed atop alpine foothills; the cliffs shoot down to steep green slopes. For mountain climbers, the park's highest peak, Mont-Aux-Sources (so named by 19th-century missionary-explorers from France) is a two-day undertaking : 10,768 feet (3,282 metres) above sea level and 28 miles of hard climbing. (Alternatively, Mont-Aux-Sources is easily accessible from the Orange Free State via Qwa Qwa. The view from the summit is stupendous.)

Royal Natal Park is inhabited by mountain antelope of several species as well as big colonies of baboons and dassies (rock-climbing little fellows resembling oversized guinea pigs). Bird-watchers have counted up to 184 species. For nature-lovers of all kinds, even city-slickers who normally walk no further than the garage, there are hiking trails and easy walks through enthralling scenery.

Giant's Castle Game Reserve, another Drakensberg wilderness, contains many fantastic rock formations. The "castle" itself—a few feet taller than Mont-Aux-Sources—is so awesome that the Africans called it "The Mountain Not To Point At". The most remarkable wildlife in this park are eland (the biggest antelope) and a giant vulture named the lammergeyer. Vultures, eagles and falcons feel perfectly at home in these mountains, as do the storm clouds which con-

With Drakensberg Amphitheatre in the distance, riders ramble over Royal Natal National Park.

Heads up! Sunflowers galore and other crops flourish between mountains and sea level in Natal.

vene for summit conferences most summer afternoons. (Which is why you shouldn't point; thunder, lightning and hail might reply.)

It's all downhill, but slowly, from Giant's Castle to the coast. About half-way, at a refreshing altitude of 3,400 feet (just over 1,000 metres), is the resort centre of **Howick**. Right on the edge of town is Howick's famous **waterfall**, a national monument. Don't bother looking for a mountain; the waterfall plunges from street level into an abyss. Many tourists stop to take pictures of the 312-foot (95-metre) falls, so urchins often lurk about the viewing area begging for coins. The place is also a noted suicide site.

From here it's about 25 kilometres south-east to the provincial capital, **Pietermaritzburg**, named after two leaders of the pioneer Voortrekkers, *Piet* Retief and Gerrit *Maritz*. The combined name is so cumbersome that some South African newspapers routinely call it Maritzburg; otherwise it's known as Sleepy Hollow. The population is about 150,000.

The founders of 1839 built wide streets, Cape-Dutch houses and gardens, but their dreams of an unfettered Boer culture quickly crashed. The town was occupied by the British in 1842. Relics of both backgrounds—Boer and British—are among Pietermaritzburg's 16 officially protected national monuments.

Pioneer mementoes—rifles, kitchen implements, and a case full of *kappies* (sun-bonnets)—are displayed in the Voortrekker Museum, a one-floor, Cape-style building from 1840, originally a church. The oldest

house in town has been moved to a site next to the museum. This thatch-roofed two-floor house, with the original tile floors and timbered ceilings from yellow-wood trees, is now a small museum in its own right.

Another proud monument is the **City Hall**, claimed to be the biggest all-brick building south of the Equator. Its elongated clock tower tells the time visually and audibly, and contains a carillon which knows several tunes.

An old-fashioned atmosphere pervades the narrow pedestrian lanes nearby, with names like Chancery Lane and Gray's Inn Lane, evoking the Inns of Court of London. Lawyers' offices have traditionally lined these back streets. This was also the financial district of Pietermaritzburg, until the local stock exchange went out of business in the depression year 1931.

The road from Pietermaritzburg to the coast at Durban is one of South Africa's really super superhighways, as notable for the dual-carriageway engineering as for the scenery. The semi-tropical countryside becomes ever more lush as the motorway descends. Closer to the metropolitan area are the hill suburbs to which Durban **55**

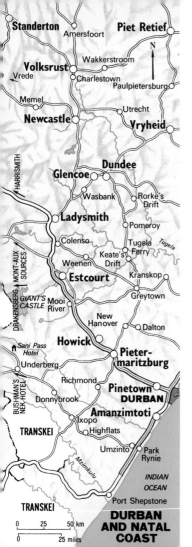

businessmen escape from the coastal heat—as appealing as any residential areas anywhere, with spacious houses embraced by bougainvillea, poinsettia and hibiscus.

About halfway to the coast the motorway passes the **Valley of a Thousand Hills**, through which the short but powerful Umgeni River journeys to the Indian Ocean. This is the same river last seen taking a shortcut at Howick Falls. The thousand (or thereabouts) hills form an inspiring panorama; haunted by the ghosts of Zulus and cannibals, cattle rustlers and pioneers, many of the hills are identified with specific legends.

This is Zulu country, and one of the tourist attractions (coach parties go from Durban) is the **Phe-Zulu tribal kraal**, which calls itself a living museum. Each of the "beehive" huts is designed to illustrate some aspect of tribal life. But the highlight for the tourists is the display of **dancing**, to the rhythm of a drum and two-toned string instruments. Topless women with big smiles compete for the most strenuous dance routine, as the tourists clap in time. The establishment's souvenir shop is crammed with topical items from cheap bead necklaces to large original carvings.

Durban

They come from all parts of South Africa to ride the surf or the roller-coaster—or a rickshaw. And somehow, Durban pulls it off, combining the "fun" atmosphere of the nation's premier beach resort with the restlessness of Africa's busiest port. Leading this year-round double life may be what keeps the city sprightly.

Durban has come a long way since 1824, when a small British trading post was planted here to barter with the powerful Zulu nation. Originally called Port Natal, the settlement was renamed in 1835 in honour of the Governor of the Cape Colony, General Sir Benjamin D'Urban. After many vicissitudes, Durban retains some aspects of England—including what may be the world's prettiest statue of an idealized Queen Victoria. And the province of Natal is the only one where the English language is used more widely than Afrikaans.

The personality of Durban is enlivened by its unique population compound: 470,000 Indians, 320,000 whites, 120,000 blacks (mostly Zulu), and 56,000 "Coloureds". More Indians live in Durban than in any other city outside India. And in Durban, although the races are separated by law, as everywhere else in South Africa, their areas are close enough together to promote a certain cosmopolitan air. Even the black townships are relatively handy to the centre of town.

For the tourist, the centre of town is the beach. Along Durban's **"Golden Mile"** run four beaches—from south to north, Addington, South, North and Battery beaches. Closest to the business district, **South Beach** is probably the most crowded. Ashore here are a children's amusement area, public bowling greens, and Durban's aquarium and dolphinarium. Performing dolphins are the stars of this show—standing on their tails, leaping through hoops and high-jumping out of the pool, to the unfailing delight of children and adults.

On the **Marine Parade** here, the last surviving rickshaws in Durban line up at a sort of taxi stand. The rickshaw was transplanted to Durban from Japan in Victorian times and soon became a popular conveyance. Now only a handful of the two-wheelers are left, and they are more for picture-taking than for transport; but in Durban they are pulled by Zulus wearing the most colourful tribal regalia. Signs at the "rickshaw rank" prescribe the proper 57

Durban skyline, more than 10 miles away, stands out behind sunbathers at Umhlanga Rocks, headquarters of Natal's shark-catchers.

price per kilometre per passenger, but the drivers try to extract more for posing for the camera.

North Beach is the hangout of surfers, thanks to the wave patterns and the profusion of pretty girls. The long, rolling waves and the comfortable sea temperature make Durban South Africa's surfing metropolis. (The whole area has been open to all races since the policy of "non-white" beaches was discontinued by the government.)

The beachfront faces east. **Victoria Embankment**, along Durban Bay, looks south. The architects who created the skyline here couldn't seem to decide whether they were inspired by Rio de Janeiro or Cleveland, Ohio. But pleasant gardens intervene all along the embankment. Here you'll find the Vasco Da Gama Clock, in a filigreed cast-iron structure, a gift from the Portuguese government in 1897.

Harbour tours and deepsea cruises depart from the

small craft harbour here. The bustling **deepwater port**—handling three times the tonnage of Cape Town, South Africa's second biggest port—always makes an interesting outing. Ships of many flags load and unload, yachts and humbler pleasure craft come and go, and you get a good look at the Durban Sugar Terminal with its three monster silos—capacity more than half a million tons. (Visitors may tour the terminal on Monday and Wednesday mornings between May and December.)

The **business district** is just a few steps inland from Victoria Embankment. The **City Hall** is said to be a pure copy version of the municipal building in Belfast—though, one has to admit the one in Northern Ireland lacks the thickets of palm trees on either side of the ceremonial portico. Opposite is Farewell Square, named after one of Durban's founders, Lieutenant Francis Farewell; this rather cluttered little park contains nearly as many statues as park benches.

Durban's British connection is graphically re-emphasized at the **General Post Office**, where a plaque recalls the arrival of a young Winston Churchill in Durban, just before Christmas in 1899. A bas-relief shows the future prime minister addressing a crowd of local residents. He had recently escaped from a Boer prisoner-of-war camp in Pretoria.

There are no plaques or statues in Durban to commemorate a contemporary of Churchill's who spent some years in the city. Mohandas K. Gandhi, non-violent fighter for Indian independence, first came to Durban in 1893 as a young lawyer. Because of his race he suffered personal indignities as petty as being evicted from a first-class railway compartment, as gross as being attacked and almost lynched by a white mob. Gandhi conceived his philosophy of non-violent defiance in South Africa, where he led mass protests against discriminatory laws. He lived in Durban on and off for 21 years.

A privately run library and **museum** devoted to the Mahatma has been established at PHOENIX, a small settlement 18 kilometres north of Durban (leave the North Coast freeway at the Kwa-Mashu exit). This is where Gandhi founded a farm collective which emphasized self-sufficiency and *satyagraha* ("firmness in truth").

The heart of Durban's Indian business district, **Grey Street**, is a most lively, exotic area to explore. Although only about 20 per cent of the local Indian population is believed to be Muslim, the Great Mosque of Grey Street is called the biggest mosque in the southern hemisphere...or at least southern Africa. The arcades of the mosque are occupied by shops selling delicacies and jewellery, saris (spelled *sarries* in Durban) and European fashions. And in the "General Herbalist" shop, with plants and roots hanging from the ceiling and piled on the floor, clients wait their turn as in a doctor's office.

The **Indian Market** in Warwick Street, a few hundred yards west of Grey Street, offers the tourist a sampling of the romance and mystery of the east. The most engaging salesmen will almost convince you to buy a lifetime supply of "hell-fire curry powder" or a home-made broom. There are Hindu religious pictures, coral, straw knickknacks...and wood and ivory carvings just off the boat from Hong Kong.

Down the street, a large, blazingly colourful fruit and vegetable market—where tourists rarely stray—is worth a roll

Housewife chooses her fish in a Durban market; Indians make up largest group in city's population.

60

or two of any photographer's film. While you're there, invest in a mango or a banana.

For a further feel of the tropics, try the Durban **Botanical Gardens**. In the orchid house there's a display of sublime orchids, tropical ferns and vines. Outside, acres of lawns are shaded by flowering, soaring, drooping, or quite incredible trees. Durban is proud of its parks, which include a formal **Japanese garden** and the **Jameson Rose Gardens,** in which 200 varieties of rose bloom in springtime (September and October).

Connoisseurs of golden beaches will enjoy the endless vistas both north and south of Durban. To reach the south coast resorts—which stretch for more than a hundred miles—you first have to travel through the port and heavy industrial areas. Eventually the scene improves to sweeping sugarlands, and finally lush subtropical vegetation interspersed with mostly empty beaches. Near Scottsburgh, **Crocworld** makes a nicely landscaped tourist attraction out of a commercial crocodile farm. The end of the line for the sleepy, not quite lovable reptiles on view here is the leather market.

Driving north out of Durban

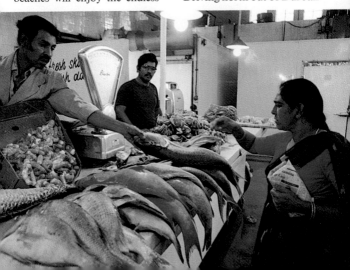

is altogether more pleasant, for the well-landscaped highway parallels the Indian Ocean. Between the sugar plantations and the sea 18 kilometres north of Durban is the picturesque resort of **Umhlanga Rocks**, with a landmark lighthouse right on the beach. This is one place the bathing should be safe, for it's the home town of the Natal Anti-Shark Measures Board.

A few of South Africa's 21,000 indigenous species of flowers scent the scene at a café in the grounds of the Durban Botanical Gardens.

Sharks Ahoy!

It's no secret: the Indian Ocean is a hotbed of sharks. And as everyone knows, it takes only one headline—"shark attacks swimmer"—to transform a prosperous resort into a deserted village. So it's economically vital, to say nothing of the humanitarian motive, to protect the beaches from the Great White Shark and other deadly species.

The grimly named Natal Anti-Shark Measures Board catches more than a thousand sharks a year just offshore. It hopes the ones that got away never come back. The board oversees more than 300 huge nets that essentially seal off 42 beaches.

Even so, the average Natal beach is closed 20 days a year. The most dangerous season is June, July and August, when universities of sardines migrate very close to the shore. This tasty prospect brings in so many sharks that the nets become clogged and damaged. If the "no swimming" sign suddenly goes up, believe it!

The Anti-Shark Measures Board is supported by the provincial treasury, but it's not a total drain on resources. The board earns some money selling shark fins, an oriental delicacy priced higher per kilo than the best steak.

The Eastern Cape Coast

From the outskirts of Cape Town to Port Elizabeth nearly 500 miles away, South Africa's southern coast is a diverting patchwork of beaches and capes, forests and lakes. For about a third of that distance the pretty Garden Route parallels the Indian Ocean. Some extraordinary natural attractions are found inland, as well —elephants and ostriches and the Cango Caves. We begin in the industrial city of Port Elizabeth and continue clockwise around the coast towards the Cape of Good Hope.

Port Elizabeth Area

South Africa's motor industry is concentrated in **Port Elizabeth,** so perhaps it's poetic justice that the very centre of the city should be violated by a mighty network of superhighways on stilts. The motorway curtain, knitted in the latest designs of flyovers and underpasses, rattles the town's tranquillity and isolates the business district from the harbour. Luckily, there's more to Port Elizabeth than first meets the eye.

For instance, there are the **beaches,** fit for a king. At least **63**

King's Beach, closest to the town centre, is where the British Royal Family took a dip during their 1947 tour of South Africa. Beyond, along Humewood Beach, the **Oceanarium complex** is an inviting mixed bag of the natural sciences. The dolphin show here is outstanding; the featured performers all originated in local waters. Next door is the snake park, where a seemingly carefree handler wraps himself in cobras, puff adders and mambas while reciting a speech on the art of avoiding snake-bites. Some 400 species of plants flourish in the sultry Tropical House. In the Night House (just inside the door of the Tropical House) the hours are reversed, so nocturnal animals you'll never see awake in a zoo go over the moon in the dim artificial light.

With a bit of imagination you can picture Port Elizabeth as it must have been 60 years ago, when the Campanile was erected. This slim bell tower 170 feet (52 metres) tall, reminiscent of the one in Venice, rings out a carillon concert every day at 8.32 a.m., 1.32 and 6.02 p.m. It may also be climbed for a view over the city and the harbour. But today the monument is almost invisible from the town, because of the motorway.

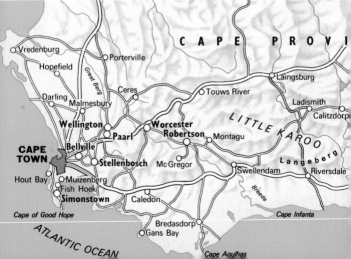

The **business district,** with big modern department stores, is what you'd expect in a city of more than half a million people. Main Street starts at the Mayor's Garden and the City Hall, a national monument dating from 1858. After a fire in 1977, the interior was redone in a sparkling modern style, though no less stately than the building's exterior. A statue of Queen Victoria, facing the harbour, marks the main public library, in which you'll also find the local tourist office.

It's a one-hour drive from Port Elizabeth, over mostly flat, often second-class roads, to the **Addo Elephant National Park.** Here the descendants of the last elephants to live wild in the Cape Province, almost extinct in the early 20th century, are thriving in loose captivity. Well over 100 elephants roam a stockade big enough to give them elbow room but small enough to better your chances of seeing one or two of them. You might also glimpse black rhino, buffalo and several types of antelope. One significant handicap to visibility, though, is the thick, evergreen Addo bush, short but impenetrable. Among all the tangled creepers and bushes are midget trees of great beauty, wonderfully garish when in flower.

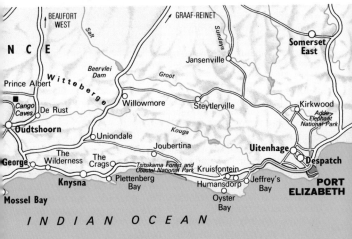

SOUTH COAST

The Garden Route: tidy towns, pink beaches and a surfer's sea.

The saga of the Addo herd won world attention in the 1920's. Stalking valuable farm land, the elephants had terrified nearby residents and damaged crops. A famous elephant hunter, Major Pretorius, was contracted to exterminate the herd. During a campaign lasting nearly a year he killed 120, but 15 of the bravest and most cunning elephants eluded him. At this point public sympathy welled up for the victims, and the survivors were reprieved.

Setting up a national park for the Addo elephants was easier than fencing them in. For years, nearby farmers filed claims for damages. Ordinary fences, however tall, were useless; the elephants pushed them over. Electrified fences were tried, but the wily beasts learned that the wooden portions held no danger, and overturned them. Automatic guns and lights to frighten any elephant touching a fence also failed. Finally, Ranger Graham Armstrong devised a high fence of tram rails secured by powerful steel cables. It works.

Eventually, the fence will enclose most of the park's 7,735 hectares (nearly 30 square miles). The elephants, still considered dangerous, are nearly back to their pre-massacre numbers. And the neighbours can relax.

Fourteen kilometres of road winds through the bush inside the enclosure, passing close to several water holes where elephants are likely to appear in dry weather. It is forbidden to get out of a car anywhere inside the stockade. Another road goes along the outside of the fence, with elevated viewing points.

The Garden Route

The N2 highway links Port Elizabeth and Cape Town. Exactly what stretch of this road deserves the semi-official title of the Garden Route is slightly vague. The most exciting section runs about 140 miles between the Storms River Mouth and Mossel Bay. Whatever its dimensions, the Garden Route is a popular tourist attraction. But don't be misled by that name: it's by no means a botanical garden bisected by a highway. It's composed of many kinds of countryside, often spectacular, but a garden only metaphorically because of its location between the desert and the sea.

Going west from Port Elizabeth, a tourist resort of note is **Jeffrey's Bay,** which calls itself South Africa's Surfing Paradise. Indeed, the rollers here are well known to the international surfing set, which arrives in March for the start of the season. At any time of year, the immense pink arc of beach is a delight. The sand is a trove of seashells, examples of which may be viewed in a **shell museum** occupying part of the library on the seafront.

In majestic countryside to the west, two national parks are centred near the Storms River. An ingenious and graceful bridge 630 feet (192 metres) long offers a formidable view down the gorge to the river far below. On the landward side of the N2 is the **Tsitsikama Forest National Park,** with trees as typical as yellow-wood, stinkwood and candlewood. Hiking trails are laid out to provide surveys of the big trees, or the ferns and lichen, or the wild flowers.

On the other side of the highway, the **Tsitsikama Coastal National Park** runs about 50 miles along the rugged, rocky Indian Ocean shore. This is the first coastal national park on the continent of Africa, a sanctuary for otter, bushbuck and vervet monkey, and 210 species of birds. The restricted zone extends half a mile into the ocean, protecting dolphins, whales and multifarious undersea creatures. A 41-kilometre hiking trail, called the Otter Trail, follows the coastline over cliffs, through forests and fording streams.

The Garden Route passes through some sensational scenery—endless stands of pine and eucalyptus behind flowering roadside trees, tortuous stretches through and over gorges, and sudden glimpses of the ocean from sheer cliffs.

When the Portuguese navigators of the 15th century saw **Plettenberg Bay** they called it Bahia Formosa (Beautiful Bay)—a judgment contemporary travellers enthusiastically share. The vast, classic arc of sandy beach is a winner with holiday-makers from near and far; a much-photographed modern hotel stands on an islet of its own; and on the hills high above are admirable villas and a neat shopping district. A highlight of this stretch of coast is the cape that protects the bay, called Robbeberg (Seal Mountain), a game reserve which is accessible on foot.

On the way from Plettenberg Bay to Knysna you may be startled to see a sign pointing out the **Garden of Eden.** Here is a chance to stretch your legs and breathe the air of the forest primeval, where the sun's rays barely filter through the interwoven branches of trees that were here long before the Portuguese first sighted the coast. Less romantically, the Forestry Department has labelled many trees for educational purposes.

The **Knysna forests**—80,000 hectares (more than 300 square miles)—are as economically valuable as they are beautiful. They were badly diminished in the 19th and early 20th centuries by reckless exploitation. With timberland comprising barely one per cent of South Africa's total area, this resource is now carefully controlled by the government. So you'll see great swathes of newly planted trees replacing those which have been felled.

The town of **Knysna** (the K is silent) is a popular tourist resort with an intriguing history. It was founded by a gentleman named George Rex, who was widely believed to be an illegitimate son of King George III of England. Rex himself—the unusual name was never explained—made no claims at all about his family background. Arriving from the Cape at the beginning of the 19th century, he bought a big farm along the Knysna lagoon and turned the district into a seaport and a ship-building and timber centre. Boats and furniture are still made in Knysna, though the port lost its commercial importance with the arrival of the railway.

A famous rocky beauty spot, "The Heads", marks the Indian Ocean's dramatic entrance into Knysna's ample lagoon, which stretches far inland The lagoon provides much cheerful scenery and a happy world for fishermen and boatsmen. One unusual landmark along the lagoon: **Holy Trinity Church** at BELVIDERE. No, it's not really a relic from Europe's Middle Ages, but a 19th-century impression of a Norman Church. It's one of the smallest churches in South Africa, with room for only 65 people.

More lagoons and lakes, cheering timberland and voluptuously moulded hills characterize the Garden Route west of Knysna. The next resort to appear bears the promising name of **The Wilderness.** What with hotels, camping sites and caravan parks, it is not as deserted as it sounds, but there are miles of unspoiled beaches.

The regional centre, **George,** was named after George Rex's putative father, the King. The most striking structure in this plateau town of 50,000 is a blinding white **Dutch Reformed Church** of the most dignified proportions. For tourists, George is most interesting for its flowers and its crucial location at the intersection of the Garden Route and a main road to the Little Karoo.

The last resort on the seaside **69**

sector of the Garden Route is **Mossel Bay,** a working seaport with some beaches and natural swimming pools among the rocks. Though sailing ships visited the bay as early as 1488, the first permanent settlement wasn't established for almost three centuries. In the meantime, passing ships often stopped for water and to trade with the local Hottentots. Sailors left messages to be relayed by other ships; the "Post Office Tree", a voluminous milkwood tree beside the fresh-water spring, was the message centre. Some letters were stuffed into old boots which were tied to the tree. So the post office has put up a boot-shaped letter box next to the tree in the municipal park overlooking the beach. Mail posted therein is given a commemorative postmark.

Herd of ostriches deploys across Little Karoo ranch; Cango Caves have 80 caverns open to public.

Little Karoo

Steam trains, turboprop planes and coach tours serve **Oudts-hoorn,** the sunny capital of the Little Karoo, a strangely beautiful semi-desert beyond the Outeniqua Mountains. It's about 35 miles inland from George.

A stroll along any shopping street in Oudtshoorn will soon show you what's different about this place. The stores sell ostrich feathers of many colours, empty ostrich eggs, dried ostrich meat, ostrich-hide wallets, even lamps and ashtrays standing upon detached ostrich feet. Restaurants advertise ostrich steaks (best served with a strong sauce) and omelets. Ostriches are big business in Oudtshoorn. Within a couple of hours you will come to know them well.

The **ostrich ranches** on the outskirts of town offer an inimitable experience. Where else could you see nature's mightiest birds by the thousand

—strutting, scratching about, or merely standing there with uncommonly vacant expressions in their bulging eyes? The guided tours of ostrich farms cover the saga in depth: the history of the Little Karoo's 90,000-strong herd, the Victorian-era boom when ostrich feathers sold for 500 rand per kilogramme, and how to go about hatching an ostrich egg. There are the ostrich races, in which the fleet, muscular non-flyers have to run with "jockeys" on their backs. And henceforth whenever you see a feather duster—or the plumage hiding a strip-tease artist—you'll know where they came from.

Why Oudtshoorn? It seems ostriches are happiest in a hot, dry climate; they like the type of alfalfa grown here for their delectation, and the availability of their favourite diet supplements—sand, stones and insects.

Twenty-six kilometres north of Oudtshoorn, in the foothills of the Swartberg ("Black Mountain"), is another of South Africa's most popular tourist attractions, the **Cango Caves.** They're easy to reach over a well-built mountain road which mostly follows a meandering river bordered with weeping willow trees. The caves originally sheltered bushmen, whose paintings were found on the walls of the entrance. Experienced guides escort the tourists into the series of chambers, pointing out the suggestive formations of stalactites and stalagmites. Wear comfortable shoes. Attached to the caves are modern amenities provided by the municipality of Oudtshoorn, including eating facilities, kennels for pets, and baby-sitters. For visiting hours, see p. 120.

72

Cape Town

One of the great moments for any traveller is the first sight of Cape Town's classic convergence of cloud-topped mountain, skyscrapered flatland and Atlantic Ocean. Like San Francisco and Rio de Janeiro, where land and sea also meet monumentally, the Mother City of South Africa gladdens the heart.

The one-and-a-half million people who live in Cape Town know they're onto a good thing. Where else could they combine the sophistication of a big city with the choice of mountain climbing or beach-combing, a couple of miles apart?

Even though the climate is suitable for pines, palms and frangipani, the locals complain

Wide-angle view from grounds of Cape Town Castle takes in Table Mountain, Lion's Head, City Hall.

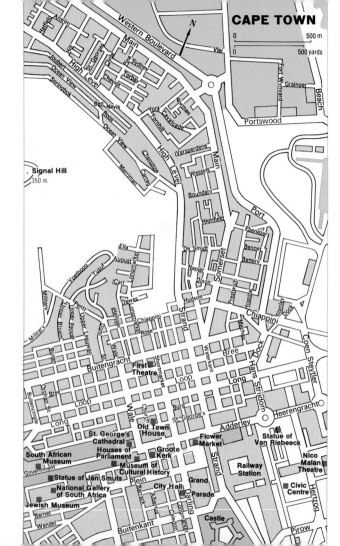

about the weather. The winters aren't terribly cold but it does rain a lot. In summer a south-easterly wind as haunting as a curse assails the city for days at a time. They call the wind the Cape Doctor, for it's credited with sweeping away germs, mosquitos, gnats and air pollution. During the "southeaster" season, Cape Town also experiences its distinctive phenomenon: the "tablecloth" atop Table Mountain—a strip of fluffy white cloud hovering over the summit, slightly draped over the edges. With or without its white mantle, Table Mountain is a cheering signpost visible to ships as far as 100 miles off (see pp. 79–80). And an all-pervasive part of the city scene.

Cape Town's main street, **Adderley Street**, runs along the sweeping modern façade of the railway terminus, where you'll find long-distance and commuter trains as well as buses to and from the airport. Between the station and the docks, the zone called the Foreshore has been reclaimed from the sea. It is occupied by an overpowering array of elevated highways and buildings designed to impress. One such building you can hardly ignore is the giant **Civic Centre**, which straddles Hertzog Boulevard; inside,

throngs of municipal officials toil. A useful part of this complex is the **Nico Malan Opera House and Theatre.** The up-to-date technology behind the scenes may be seen on guided tours of the theatres.

Seagulls and sea breezes tell you the harbour is very near. But Cape Town's port is so big it's best explored by car. Better yet, take one of the **harbour cruises** for the flavour of banana boats, fishing trawlers and container leviathans.

Adderley Street pedestrians are funneled underground on the landward side of the railway station. In the passage beneath Strand Street, the local tourist information office offers maps, brochures and accommodation advice. Also in the underground concourse, under glass, is an old "postal stone" under which 17th-century sailors placed letters to be picked up by homeward-bound ships.

An alley off Adderley Street, **Trafalgar Place**, is the site of Cape Town's outdoor flower market. The sales personnel here are jolly women of Cape Town's Malay community. The Cape Malays are mostly the descendants of slaves brought in from Asia in the second half of the 17th century. They are Muslims and live **75** in a separate neighbourhood, fortuitously close to the business district (beyond Buitengracht Street). **The Malay Quarter** is worth a visit for the sight of the pastel-coloured little houses, the minarets, and the kindly people themselves. Muslims of Indian extraction also live in this district.

By far the majority of the population of Cape Town is officially classified as "Coloured", that is, of mixed race. They outnumber the whites nearly two to one. Most are descended from intermarriages involving early white settlers, Hottentots, indigenous blacks or imported slaves. The black population of Cape Town is small, amounting to one out of every eight residents. Most are Xhosa speakers; listen for the amazing clicking sounds which pop up in their conversations.

Cape Town City Hall, a very large Italian Renaissance palace from the turn of the 20th century, faces the **Grand Parade**, which used to be a parade ground for troops. Before that, the Dutch East India Company's very first building in the Cape settlement stood on this spot—an earthwork fort of 1652. Now the Parade is a big car park, relieved by a fruit and flower market and, every Wednesday and Saturday

morning, a flea market. While you're eyeing the pseudo-antiques and bargain-priced clothing, beware of the pickpockets who keep busy here.

Beyond the Grand Parade stands the **Castle of Good Hope**, a sturdy, pentagon-shaped fortress, now surrounded by inviting gardens. You may be surprised to see modern soldiers marching and saluting within these venerable stone walls; the Castle is the headquarters of the Western Cape Command of the South African Defence Forces. Military personnel lead guided tours of the Castle six times a day, recounting its history, explaining the tactical layout, and showing off the dungeons. The Castle contains small military and maritime museums as well as the William Fehr Collection of paintings, Cape silver and furniture, and Asian porcelain.

Facing the cobbled **Greenmarket Square**, the **Old Town House** is a grand baroque building from 1761, that served as the city hall until 1905. Now the green-shuttered white building holds the Michaelis Collection of Dutch and Flemish art. The heart of the exhibition is the art produced in the mother country at the time of the original Cape settlement: a treasured Frans Hals portrait and

An eastern mirage seems to haunt this street in central Cape Town, part of the exotic Malay Quarter.

dozens of oils by his contemporaries.

The **Groote Kerk** ("Great Church"), where Adderley Street runs into the pedestrians-only Government Avenue, is sometimes, debatably, called the oldest church in South Africa. It is, at least, the best known. The original Dutch Reformed church at this location was built in the 17th century, and the present clock tower dates from 1703. The bulk of the building was rebuilt considerably later.

Government Avenue, an oak-shaded gravel walk over half a mile long, is a restful place for a stroll in central Cape Town. It runs down the middle of the original Dutch East India Company's Garden, laid out by the first governor, Jan Van Riebeeck. Here some 300 slaves produced fruits and vegetables for settlers and the visiting ships of the Company. About one-third of the original farm area has been turned into a resplendent botanical garden; the rest is occupied by buildings as important as the South African Houses of Parliament. **77**

Several cultural institutions surround the Company's Garden: the **South African National Gallery** emphasizes the work of South African artists; there is also a strong showing of English painters.

The **Jewish Museum** nearby occupies the Greek-columned building of South Africa's first synagogue (1862); next door is the present, twin-towered Gardens Synagogue.

The **South African Museum**, the oldest such institution in the country, has dioramas of prehistoric life in Southern Africa and a valuable collection of rock paintings of animals by bushmen artists.

Table Mountain

People have been climbing Table Mountain since at least 1503, when the Portuguese mariner Antonio de Saldanha went up to check the lie of the land—and sea. Nowadays climbers can choose from about 350 routes to the 3,567-foot (1,087-metre) summit of the shale, granite and sandstone flat-top. But the climb can be dangerous, so amateurs are warned to start early, be

18th-century Town House keeps all its dignity amidst skyscrapers.

certain of the weather, and dress for the occasion (sensible shoes, and carry some warm clothing, just in case).

Or, you can go up the easy, safe way—in seven minutes. The Table Mountain Aerial Cableway Company has been whisking passengers to the top, and back again, since 1929. Every year about 250,000 sightseers take the trip, thrilling to the swaying ride and the view. There's plenty of room for roaming on the rocky summit, and maps and telescopes for taking your bearings. If the weather begins to deteriorate, a siren goes off to warn the visitors to assemble at the cableway station for a return to earth before service is suspended.

In good weather the cars operate half-hourly between 8.30 a.m. and 6 p.m. (until 10.30 p.m. in summer). If you're using public transport, take the city bus marked "Kloof Nek" from Adderley Street. A small bus operated by the Cableway Company takes you the rest of the way to the lower cable terminus.

Photographers requiring a spectacular picture of Table Mountain may want to sign up for an aerial tour of the peninsula. Check with the local tourist office, Captour, or the local airline, Air Cape. An- 79 other way to do it is by driving northwards around Table Bay on the M14 highway. Just past the Ascot race course, the road closes in on the infinite sand dunes along the Atlantic.

Across the water is your impeccable, head-on view of the mighty cliff in Cape Town's life, accompanied by the familiar silhouettes of Devil's Peak and Lion's Head.

Legendary Table Mountain seen from a beach north of Cape Town; Opposite page: Duiker Island, home for hundreds of sunbathing seals.

The Cape Peninsula

The Cape of Good Hope is as gripping a part of the world as you'll ever see, and the sights on the way are worth stopping for—even if it isn't the exact spot where Atlantic and Indian oceans collide.

There are two likely routes for an excursion around the 50-kilometre-long peninsula. The more leisurely itinerary goes around the coast, counter-clockwise from central Cape Town, past South Africa's oldest working lighthouse at **Green Point.**

Sea Point is an in-town beach resort with a fashionable sea-front promenade and high-rent high-rises of every imaginable architectural style. For miles beyond, the road reveals beach after inviting beach, alternating with rocky coves. **Clifton Bay** is most popular, with four beaches; each has its own character and clientele—from families with children to surfers and girls in tangas. The sunbathing season is at its height from mid-October to mid-March. All along the Atlantic coast, however, the water is cold the year round. For tolerable sea temperatures you have to go to the opposite shore of the peninsula and the tangibly warmer waters of False Bay.

The coast road soon turns inland along the slopes of the mountain formation known as the Twelve Apostles (actually, a continuation of the back of Table Mountain), with invigorating land-and-sea scenery. When the highway finally returns to sea level, it's at the big semicircular fishermen's har-

bour of **Hout Bay**. Although some yachts are parked here, Hout Bay is obviously a working port. At certain times of the year the industrial aspects overwhelm the scenery, for the fish-processing factories emit heady vapours. The end products are fish meal and fish oil. Hout Bay is also a major source of a tasty South African delicacy, smoked *snoek*, and the coveted crustacean known as crayfish (or rock lobster abroad).

A favourite excursion from here is by launch to some rocks called Duiker Island, out beyond the calm of the harbour. Hundreds of seals may be seen at work and play, the youngsters being cajoled into the sea to learn how to cope, the old-timers lolling like itchy sunbathers searching for a comfortable position on the rocks. Birds—cormorants, gulls and oyster-catchers—perch wing to wing on available spaces.

Beyond Hout Bay the Marine Drive rises to its greatest achievement, a corniche-road of world-class beauty, barely hanging between the cliffs and the sea. When Chapman's Peak Drive was undertaken at the time of World War I, it was considered a daring breakthrough in road engineering. A lookout point is considerably provided at the highest spot on the drive.

The route soon swerves inland and crosses the Cape Peninsula, now scarcely 6 miles wide. At the eastern extremity is the small town of **Fish Hoek**, known far and wide throughout South Africa as the country's only "dry" community. Bars and liquor stores have been forbidden here since the early 19th century. The beach is terribly respectable, too.

The other way to go from Cape Town to Fish Hoek (almost the threshold of the Cape of Good Hope) is the inland route, which is also scenic. The M3 highway leaves town as a busy but nicely landscaped boulevard. Cast a glance at the sprawling "campus" of Groote Schuur Hospital. History was made here in 1967: Professor Christiaan Barnard led the team which performed the first transplant of a human heart. Across the road, deer graze.

On the slopes of Devil's Peak, the **Rhodes Memorial** honours the financier/statesman with a monument as pompous as any emperor could desire: in a simulated Greek Temple at the top of a cascade of granite steps, a bust of Cecil Rhodes looks pensively out over what was, in life, his favourite panorama.

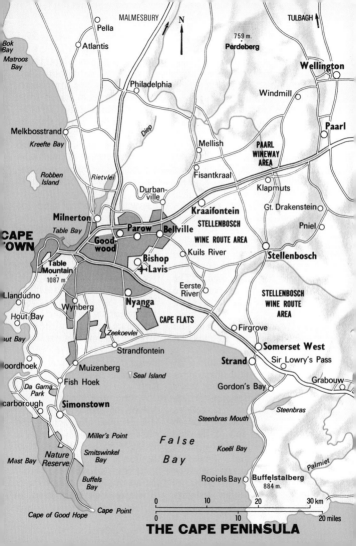

THE CAPE PENINSULA

South Africa's oldest university occupies a priceless forested setting under Devil's Peak. The University of Cape Town, founded in 1829, has both ivy-covered traditional buildings and stark new ones. The new Baxter Theatre here is an intellectual focus of the city as well as the university.

About 3 kilometres past the U.C.T. campus, it's a short sidetrip off the M3 to **Kirstenbosch**, a renowned botanical garden. Thousands of species of plants grow here—nearly one-fourth of all the types found in South Africa. (Because of the varied climates, no single botanical garden can cover the entire national range.) The Western Cape is considered South Africa's flower garden, and Kirstenbosch is its showplace. August, September and early October are the most exciting times here.

Dramatic landscaping adds to the impact of the old country seats of the Cape—big white houses, often thatch-roofed, which manage to be refined and sparkling. Cape Dutch architecture is full of likeable touches: symmetrical gables with curves and sometimes baroque intricacies; window shutters, perhaps covering the bottom half alone; haughty main doors with fan-lights; and, inside, airy rooms with timbered ceilings. One of the most magnificent Cape Dutch houses, called **Groot Constantia**, south of Kirstenbosch, is now a museum. Great wines were produced on this farm beginning at the turn of the 18th century. Part of the old cellars, behind the main house, has been turned into a small wine museum. The main museum, occupying the homestead itself, displays antique furniture, glassware, porcelain and implements.

The name False Bay makes it seem some kind of imposter, like a peninsula posing as an island. **False Bay** really is a bay, about 30 kilometres wide, with many miles of tantalizing beaches. Some early navigators, returning from the Indian Ocean, mistook it for the open Atlantic and made a hard right turn. Then they had to wait for a wind to extricate them. That's all that's false about False Bay.

A booming resort on this side of the coast, **Muizenberg**, first attracted attention in 1899 when Cecil Rhodes bought a holiday cottage there. Now thousands of holiday-makers come from all over the republic to fan out over endless dunes of almost-snow-white sand. In summer the prevailing south-easterly winds tend to pump the tepid waters of the Mozambique Current into False Bay, ousting the Atlantic chill. It's quite swimmable from November to April.

The suburban railway from Cape Town runs out to SIMONSTOWN, the main base of the South African navy. Ship spotters can see frigates and minesweepers here, and perhaps a submarine... along with many an enviable yacht. A most unusual monument to Simonstown's history as a British naval base is a **Martello Tower**, rather hidden inside the dockyard area. This cylindrical stone fort, built in 1796, is thought to be the oldest of its kind in the world. It's been restored and turned into a small museum of naval mementoes.

In 1488 the dauntless Portuguese explorer Bartholomew Dias rounded the cape but he couldn't see it for the storm. On his map he wrote, "Cape of Storms". On the return trip, though, Dias saw the cape in the sunshine. What a difference! That's when he re-named it the Cape of Good Hope.

Even though lighthouses, paved roads and a restaurant have been added, the **Cape of Good Hope Nature Reserve** remains a wonderland, virtually intact in its primeval state. Driving slowly and attentively along the lesser roads you might come across eland, springbok, ostrich and other wildlife on the hoof. The baboons, unfortunately, are legion. Signs in several languages warn visitors they face a nasty fine for feeding the apes. (And remember to lock your car with the windows closed, for baboons routinely loot unlocked vehicles.) Specialists are fascinated by the reserve's flora—mostly low shrubs and grass. Laymen will enjoy the outbursts of colour from wild protea and heather.

The reserve's 25 miles of coastline varies from cliffs to rocky flats and sandy coves. But the high-spot is where the roads run out, at **Cape Point**. A small bus called the Flying Dutchman shuttles visitors from the car park to the top of the final hill. From there you can walk to various observation points, the highest set up at the base of the original 1860 lighthouse. You can't see the present, very powerful lighthouse from here; it's far down the point in hopes the beacon will be visible beneath the fog.

At Cape Point the granite cliffs plunge 850 feet (259 metres) to the sea—South Africa's tallest sea cliffs. Giant rollers froth at the base of the "skyscraper" of stone, while cormorants fight the shrieking wind to find their ledges. Albatross, gannets, gulls and giant petrels share the fishing ground of this tormented sea.

Looking west from the Cape Point lookout positions you see the Cape of Good Hope itself, a less dramatic physical feature than Cape Point but actually the southwesternmost point of Africa. The spot is accessible from the road, so you can climb the rocks near sea level for a close look at breakers lashing the shore. This is the specific headland which gave the whole peninsula its name.

Wine Country

South African wines, which can hold their own against almost any overseas competition, originate in a small corner of the country, within a hundred-mile radius of Cape Town. The soils and micro-climates are so varied within this arc that all manner of wines can be produced—whites, rosés, reds, sherries and ports.

The two principal wine regions, Stellenbosch and Paarl, are covered in a single day's excursion offered by the tour operators. Or you can do it

yourself at a more leisurely pace. The tourist information offices of both regions issue voluminous brochures, maps and suggested itineraries. Aside from the educational benefits, the tastings are fun and the scenery is enchanting.

Stellenbosch, less than 50 kilometres due east of central Cape Town, has more beautiful old buildings than any other municipality in South Africa. It's an endearing university town, as relaxed as the students going to lectures on their bikes.

The town is named after that great 17th-century wine booster, Governor Van der Stel. We can thank him for the

layout of the streets and the rows of great oaks. But fires destroyed the original, thatch-roofed cottages. The best of the buildings on view today were put up between 1775 and 1820. They're all different but compatible, on the same scale, whitewashed and delightful.

An 18th-century mansion with a prize-winning garden, **Grosvenor House**, is filled with authentic Old Cape furnishings. Another museum, **Schreuder House**, is in what's called the oldest surviving town house in South Africa; it is furnished as a simple settler's cottage of an earlier day. A homestead of 1780 now houses the **Rembrandt Van Rijn Art Gallery**. In the same compound, a wine museum displays old Roman amphoras and antique glasses and bottles. Nearby, a **brandy museum** illustrates the history and technology of brandy making. (The building, which blends smoothly with its aged neighbours, is less than a century old, designed by Sir Herbert Baker.)

Cliffhanger: sea birds make their home in Cape Point ledges, high above the boiling Atlantic surf at the south-western tip of Africa.

Surrounding Stellenbosch, in an area with a Mediterranean aspect, vineyards are spread over hillsides and on the flat, with imposing mountains as a background. About 15 **wine estates** and co-operatives in the district welcome visitors, usually with scheduled cellar tours, wine tastings and sales —daily except Saturday afternoons and Sundays. Most of the firms have their headquarters in handsome white homesteads in idyllic settings.

The "capital" of the other wine region, **Paarl,** is about 60 kilometres from Cape Town, just off the N1 motorway, which features miles of flowering shrubs down the dividing island.

Paarl is about twice the size of Stellenbosch, though you may think it's even bigger when you see the massive modern civic centre, in which the tourist information office operates. But Paarl is an old town with a winning atmosphere. The endless main street—absolutely unwalkable—is lined with historic buildings and working vineyards. Right on Main Street is the headquarters of KWV, the Ko-operatiewe Wijnbouwers-Vereniging (Co-operative Wine Growers Association). Tours are scheduled four times a day.

The Old Parsonage Museum occupies a perfectly restored 18th-century Cape Dutch building. Authorities on Old Cape furniture and silver consider the exhibits here among the finest in the country.

Elsewhere in Paarl and the surrounding Berg River Valley are half a dozen **wine estates** and 10 co-operative cellars. Most have wines for sale, with or without tastings, and cellar tours either on a schedule or by arrangement.

A superlative view of the town, the vineyards and the nearby mountains may be had from the site of the **Taalmonument** (language monument), high on a hilltop above the southern outskirts of Paarl. From a distance the monument seems to hang over the town like a family of stalagmites, but on closer view it's a much more complex and ingenious work of abstract art. The idea of honouring a language with a monument would not occur to most nations, but the Afrikaners cling to theirs with a fierce pride.

Classic Cape Dutch architecture: historic Boschendal, built in 1812 in wine area east of Cape Town.

The Blue Train

The most luxurious 1,608-kilometre railway journey in the world must be the Blue Train's 26-hour voyage between Cape Town and Pretoria via Johannesburg. Even travellers accustomed to first-class travel are impressed with this five-star hotel-and-restaurant on wheels. Here is a train with a three-room suite: a lounge, bedroom, bathroom and toilet. Taking a bath—not a shower but a real bath—at 100 kilometres per hour is not the sort of experience the clients of British Rail or Amtrak can look forward to.

Passengers in simpler quarters, even those who have to share the shower facilities, still enjoy the general air-conditioned air of well-being. When they built this train in 1972, the planners of South African Railways thought of everything: the thin layer of gold on the glass of the double windows reduces heat and glare; the venetian blinds between the panes operate electrically; the air springs and extra insulation guarantee a quiet, smooth ride. Huge bouquets of fresh strelitzia, protea and orchids decorate the bar car, with a cornucopia of fresh fruit in the restaurant.

The congenial party—106 passengers and 26 crew members— starts out as glamorously as the old ocean liner sailings. People come down to the train to see off friends and relatives, and free champagne is distributed for brief on-board going-away parties. After the last-minute excitements and flagwaving, the 16-car train eases into motion almost imperceptibly, and of course punctually. Electricity powers the train for most of the trip, but diesel locomotives handle the central section between Beaufort West and Kimberley.

When the train stops for the switch of locomotives or a ten-minute technical stop, passengers stroll the platform like sailors regaining their sea-legs. Otherwise, there's not much to do but lounge about the bar car (the stools are bolted down but the armchairs can be moved) and eat the many-coursed meals (food is included in the ticket price).

But sightseeing from the train has its gratifications: Table Mountain, the Paarl vineyards, desert landscapes only a rattlesnake could love. During the triumphal crossing of the Hex River Mountains the sinuous track offers home-movie cameramen the chance to film the front and rear of the train from the middle. The approach to Johannesburg is announced by the sight of truncated pyramids of the slag-heaps of gold mines.

Reservations for the Blue Train open 11 months in advance, but late cancellations do happen.

What to Do

Sports

Half the country seems to be armed with fishing rods, cricket bats or surfboards. The other half is watching rugby, wrestling or racing. National monuments like golfer Gary Player or cricket star Graham Pollack tend to get more publicity and acclaim than mere film celebrities, much less politicians.

Ignoring two oceans, angler tries for a prize in a mountain stream.

Water Sports

Fishermen, whether they prefer rock, surf or deep-sea **fishing**, have a field day in South Africa. Everything an angler could dream of may be found in the South Atlantic and Indian oceans. And where they meet, near Cape Town, is said to be the home of more kinds of game fish than any other sea; for instance, all species of marlin and tunny (tuna) have been landed there.

In the big ports like Cape Town and Durban, organized **deep-sea excursions** are advertised. Elsewhere, small, powerful ski-boats may be hired to reach the action.

The best seasons for rock and surf fishing vary with the region. In the south-western Cape, it's January to April, but along the Natal coast the most promising time is from June to November. Unparalleled excitement arrives in June between Port St. Johns and Durban. Immense shoals of sardines run along the coast, sometimes being driven ashore by the waves. The sardines attract hordes of shark, barracuda, kingfish and shad, which in turn

Durban surfers can find worthy waves right on the home front.

lure fleets of happy anglers to the scene.

South Africa's 1,800-odd miles of **beaches** offer sea, sand and seashells for all tastes. In some parts of Natal and the Cape, dunes stretch endlessly into total wilderness. If you prefer convenience and companionship, there are popular resorts with all facilities. Because

92

where the big rollers also satisfy.

Sailboarding, or windsurfing, is the fastest-growing water sport in South Africa, from the warm Indian Ocean to the chill Atlantic (where wet-suits are standard attire) and on lakes and dams between the oceans.

Old-fashioned **sailing** hasn't lost its allure. There are 90 yacht clubs, where round-the-world boatsmen can find kindred, salty souls.

Sports Ashore

Golf has been played in South Africa for well over a century. Hundreds of the country's courses welcome foreign tourists, at least on weekdays. There are also public courses in Johannesburg and Durban; even these are not normally overcrowded. Of course golf goes on year-round, but some seasons are better than others. Over most of the country, the greens are at their greenest in southern summer (December to March)...but take an umbrella for that afternoon thunderstorm.

Mild weather also enhances the year-round **tennis** possibilities. The Wimbledon of South Africa, Ellis Park in Johannesburg, has 21 courts. The city has over 170 tennis clubs, including the Wanderers, with

of sharks and tricky tides, be sure to swim only where signs indicate it's safe. The busier beaches have lifeguards on duty.

Surfing, a Hawaiian invention, has become as South African as golf or rugby. The waves of the Eastern Cape are fit for champions, with absolutely impeccable conditions at Cape St. Francis and Jeffrey's Bay. Two-thirds of all the surfers in South Africa are said to come from the Durban area,

26 courts. Most resort hotels countrywide either have their own courts or access to facilities nearby.

The tranquil British game of **bowls** arrived in South Africa a century ago, slowly spreading inland from Port Elizabeth to the Rand. Today 60,000 bowlers belong to some 800 clubs; visiting players from abroad are always welcomed.

Horseback riding and associated sports go on all over the republic. The Johannesburg area alone counts 20 riding schools with more than a thousand horses. Out in the wilds, some country hotels have their own stables. Pony treks are arranged in the Drakensberg mountains.

Race meetings are held year-round. The major tracks are in Johannesburg, Cape Town, Port Elizabeth, Bloemfontein and Durban. The race of the year is the Durban July Handicap, ten and a half furlongs run on the first Saturday of

July, a social and sporting event keenly followed by all South Africans.

The glamour highlight of the **motor racing** season is the South African Grand Prix at Kyalami, north of Johannesburg, where the Formula One stars reach 320 kilometres per hour on the thoroughly revamped racetrack. A whole weekend of warm-ups and entertainment surrounds the big event.

Other popular **spectator**

Great outdoors: bowls along the ocean, hiking in Drakensberg.

sports are rugby, soccer, cricket, boxing, wrestling and athletics.

Saturday is the biggest day for organized sports in South Africa. Until very recent times Sunday sport of any importance was banned under the strict Sabbath observance laws, but major breaches of the taboo have now become almost routine.

Shopping

The gifts you can buy in South Africa range from primitive to sophisticated, from ridiculously cheap to horrendously expensive. The shops are comparably diverse. There are flea markets and quaint bazaars and women squatting on the pavement selling the baskets they weave. And there are air-conditioned boutiques with polyglot sales personnel and big-city shopping centres vast enough for hours of browsing.

One South African eccentricity: you may see a sign in a shop's door: "Closed Owing to Weather. Come In." It means the door, not the shop, is closed to keep out some unseasonable wind or rain; normally many shops keep their doors open.

What to Buy—A to Z

African curios. No end to the supply of tribal shields, spears and masks, mostly produced by the manual equivalent of assembly lines. Some of the more artistic designs come from other countries, so it's pertinent to ask the origin.

Beads. Early traders from Europe gave glass beads to the indigenous Africans in exchange for ivory or other valuable commodities. Now European tourists are buying beadwork in bright geometric designs. Each colour and design has a significance. Very inexpensive necklaces, dolls and ornaments.

Butterfly pictures. Each picture comes with a disclaimer assuring that no butterfly has suffered during the process of creation; tiny parts of wings of different colours are assiduously glued together to form a coherent African scene.

Chess sets. Figurines of African warriors are the pawns, medicine men the bishops, and so on.

Diamonds. This is where they come from, so you might consider picking up a bauble. Jewellers licensed by the South African Customs give duty-free preference to bona-fide foreign tourists on cut, ground, polished but un-set diamonds. Semi-precious stones, which also abound here, come closer to most budgets: agate, amethyst, jasper, rose quartz, verdite, etc.

Flowers. South Africa's national flower, the Protea, may be carried home, preserved and boxed with pampas grass and other typical flora.

Indian spices. Curry powder and chilli peppers with explosive colours and names, jars of chutney and all the fixings are likely souvenirs of Durban.

Ivory. Elephant tusks legitimately obtained from the culled herds of the Kruger Park are carved into little animals or busts of African figures. But note that most countries now ban the importation of ivory.

Jewellery. Certain jewellers with special customs licences are able to sell gold pendants, chains, earrings, cufflinks and such to visitors without charging the stiff South African duty. You have to show your passport, air ticket and flight reservation.

Krugerrands. Collectors of gold will always be pleased to receive one, or a set, of these desirable South African coins which are, after all, much more portable than old-fashioned ingots. They may be purchased duty-free for foreign currency in the departure hall of Johannesburg's Jan Smuts airport.

Musical instruments. You'll soon learn to play one of those small bush xylophones of metal spikes and a carved wooden base. You can also take home a small drum-rattle for rhythm accompaniment, or a big carved drum to thump.

Shopping for "African curios" in Cape Town: don't be afraid to ask where the goods come from.

Ostrich eggs. Gaily painted or *au naturel,* these jumbos are certainly conversation-starters. Even more useful are ostrich-skin wallets and handbags.

Pottery. Talented African artisans produce coiled pots with ancient tribal designs or thrown pots with new, original motifs.

Rugs and tapestries. Hand-woven in geometric or figurative designs, these are suitable for wall-hangings or carpets. From spinning wheel to final trimming, these works of rural art are produced with meticulous care.

Saris. Try an off-the-peg model when you're in Durban.

Seashells and coral. Those 1,800 miles of beach turn up

On the spicy side of the street: shoppers at Durban's Indian Market are offered "Mother-in-Law curry powder", chilli peppers and chutney.

seashells which serious collectors covet. Coral fantasies are also sold in curio shops on the coast and inland.

Stinkwood souvenirs. The fine-grained South African hardwood makes solid furniture and pretty carvings. Have a sniff: stinkwood only smells when it's freshly cut.

Straw goods. Bags, baskets, mats and trays are sold in souvenir shops or by the roadside.

Wines. Export-quality wines, sherries, ports and brandies make a natural and useful souvenir of the Cape.

Woodcraft. Salad bowls, meat trays, spoons and ladles. Wood sculptures run from cute miniature rhinos to an elaborate carving of a whole tribe of figures climbing a tree-trunk.

Zebra skins. Stripes for your wall or floor reach reputable shops from authorized game-park sources. Much less expensive are the antelope skins, of which handbags and wallets and cushion-covers are made.

Entertainment

The big cities and resort towns have discos and supper clubs, mostly in or near the major hotels. On weekdays, the festivities may go on until 2 or 3 a.m., but on Saturday nights everything shuts down at midnight. South Africa's Sabbath observance laws decree no dancing, no bars, not even plays or film shows on Sunday. (But the tribal dancing shows by gold miners are permitted in Johannesburg, and classical music concerts also evade the ban.)

The regulations governing alcohol are very likely to confuse the foreign visitor. For instance, while bars are closed on Sundays, properly licensed res-

taurans are permitted to serve beer or wine with meals. Compared with the proliferation of pubs in Britain, bars in general are rare in South Africa. Normally they are for white men only. There are "Ladies' Bars", theoretically more refined, where white women and men are served. In the port cities, the sailors' bars are considerably less dignified.

The culturally uplifting aspects of South Africa have much to offer. Lively professional theatres present plays in English or Afrikaans. Well qualified ballet, symphony and opera companies, maintained with provincial blessings, present their work in the most comfortable and technically advanced theatres and opera houses.

Cinemas show current international releases, though erotic films are either edited or prohibited. There are several performances daily, with advanced booking. In Johannesburg, Pretoria and Cape Town, tickets to films as well as plays and concerts may be bought at branches of Computicket, a computerized booking agency.

Johannesburg gold miners display skills for Sunday tourists.

Dining Out

With 13-million head of cattle on South African prairies and two oceans to provide the fish, you're assured of good, wholesome food in abundance. Your only complaint may be the exaggerated size of the portions. In many restaurants "doggy bags" are called for, in the American way, so that the excess can be taken home for future use; you don't have to prove you own a pet.

The wine part of the equation is something to cheer about: creditable domestic wines at reasonable prices.

In the big cities, restaurants come in almost all sorts, from five-star shrines of haute-cuisine and elegance down to the most utilitarian hamburger-and-pizza pit. Johannesburg claims to have restaurants of 20 nationalities—if you count "international" and vegetarian as nationalities. Cape Town has typical restaurants dealing in old Cape Dutch recipes. Durban is noted for its Indian restaurants, though many of the spices have to be imported because they won't grow in monsoon-free South Africa. All along the coasts you'll find fish restaurants which clearly have good connections down at the harbour. Establishments calling themselves cafés are, by the standards of the rest of the world, nothing of the sort. You can buy takeaway food and soft drinks in a South African café, but there's nowhere to sit down and have coffee or tea, much less a meal.

If you're in a hotel, breakfast may be included in the price. Even if it's not, this is one meal that's usually a bargain. A typical lineup would include fresh fruit and juice, hot or cold cereals, an awfully British fish dish such as kippers or poached haddock, bacon or sausage or kidneys, eggs, toast and rolls, butter and marmalade, tea or coffee. Many hotels have breakfast buffets in the Scandinavian manner, though the tastes are more English. They even cool the toast on toast-racks.

Another British tradition: most hotels send coffee or tea to your room in lieu of a wake-up call.

At Kruger National Park it's customary to take coffee or tea at dawn, then go out on safari, returning for a hearty breakfast in mid-morning.

From the Ocean
Most restaurants, specialists or not, have fish on the menu, usually fresh. A few typical South African fishes:

Cape salmon is a tasty white-meat fish which is unrelated to the big fish known as salmon in Europe and North America. *Kabeljou* is similar to cod. *Kingklip,* a large, meaty fish, makes fine fillets. *Snoek,* a cold-water fish about a yard long, is served smoked as a starter or grilled as a main event. *Steenbras* resembles sea bream. Stockfish, a member of the hake family, is said to be the most frequently trawled fish of all.

Look for the excellent shell-fish: fresh oysters, mussels, *perlemoen* (abalone), prawns (the latter often imported from Australia). Local crayfish (the correct name is crawfish or spiny rock lobster) is an expensive delicacy for a big night out.

The Meat Course
South Africa's favourite food is *braaivleis* (barbecued meat), the sort of feast the family cooks up in the garden or at a picnic spot. The whole business is taken very seriously indeed: special cuts of meat are sold for this purpose, and hardwood is selected for its proper fire-making qualities.

Unless you are invited to a *braai,* you'll have to taste an approximation in one of the many steak-houses. The steaks

—fillet, rump, sirloin, tournedos or T-bone—are invariably big, thick and tender. Whether you ask for it or not, the cook is liable to grill it with a barbecue sauce. A number of other sauces are usually on the menu, the most piquant being "monkey gland" sauce (tabasco and chutney are the surprise ingredients).

In steak houses and other restaurants you'll also find a variety of alternate main courses: lamb, veal, pork, poultry and game.

Chef lends a gloved hand at South African-style smorgasbord.

Here are some traditional South African meat dishes:

Bobotie, a baked minced-meat recipe from the Cape, with hints of apricot, almond, chutney and curry, may come from Malaya. *Boerewors* are flavourful country sausages, usually of a beef and pork combination. *Bredie* is a rich ragout, usually of mutton, with a thick tomato sauce. *Sosaties* are kebabs with a Malayan zing—chunks of lamb marinated in vinegar, sugar, garlic, curry powder and apricot.

All dishes come with potatoes (usually chips—french fries) and cooked vegetables —whatever's in season: beans, broccoli, carrots, mushrooms, pumpkin, squash or *mealies* (corn-on-the-cob). Steak houses and some other restaurants may have salad bars in the American style—a big choice of nutritious raw vegetables and dressings to combine according to whim.

Desserts

If you're still going strong, look over the sweets—apple pie, *melktert* (pastry and custard), a trifle (sponge cake soused in fruits, nuts, custard and whipped cream), or crêpes Suzette. Fresh fruit is a special treat when it's just in from the plantation—small, naturally sweet pineapples, bananas of various sizes and grades, melons, apples, grapes. And look for home-made ice cream of real fruit flavours.

For cheese lovers, there are a number of good South African imitations of the most interesting European cheeses—brie, camembert, cheddar, gouda, mozzarella, and so on—hardly distinguishable from the originals except that the price here is lower.

Before you've finished your dessert the waiter, unbidden, will probably present you with the bill. In South Africa this is considered a courtesy, intended to show the customer how attentive the staff is. It is not intended to push you out of the restaurants. However, South Africans rarely linger over their food.

South African Wines

Cape wines have come a long way. The vineyards of the early settlers were planted with the classic grapes of the Old World. But the same plague that ravaged European grapes in the 1880's struck South Africa, and the vineyards had to be replenished with immune American grafts.

So the names of the grapes are mostly familiar: Riesling, Chardonnay, Sylvaner among the whites, and Cabernet, Pinot Noir, Gamay and Zinfandel for the reds. In addition, there are two native South African varieties: Steen is a delicate mystery, perhaps a natural mutation of Sauvignon Blanc, and highly successful in sweet and dry white, rosé and champagne-style wines. The other innovation is called Pinotage, a cross between Pinot Noir and Hermitage (Cinsaut), which has proved a success in full red wines.

Aside from wine, there are European-style beers (served very cold), international brands of soft drinks (called ''cooldrinks''), mineral water and many flavours of delicious fruit juices. In a pinch, it's not unfashionable to ask for tap water—potable everywhere.

N.B. Many restaurants lack wine or liquor licences: check in advance. South Africans often arrive at licenceless restaurants with their own wine. The confused foreigner is likely to be left out in the cold; for one thing, wine shops only operate during normal shopping hours and never on Sundays... Still, kindly waiters just might bend the law for innocents abroad.

Testing local vintages and snacks on the Stellenbosch wine route.

BLUEPRINT for a Perfect Trip

How to Get There

Although the fares and conditions described below have all been carefully checked, it is advisable to consult a travel agent for the latest information.

Scheduled Flights

You can fly to South Africa from North America and Canada via a number of European cities, including Athens, London, Frankfurt, Lisbon, Rome and Zurich.

There are direct flights from Heathrow to Johannesburg, and non-stop flights to Cape Town, where a connecting service is offered to Cape Town, Durban, Port Elizabeth and other cities. European airlines also operate services to Cape Town, Durban and Windhoek.

Charter Flights and Package Tours

From North America: All-inclusive package tours are available. Costs covered include round-trip air fare (usually from New York), accommodation, most or all meals, transfers, baggage handling, local transportation and sightseeing.

From Great Britain: Tour operators offer a variety of holidays with everything included, plus land-only packages if you wish to arrange your own air travel. Certain airlines can obtain hotel and car-hire discounts for their passengers. The South African Tourism Board (see TOURIST INFORMATION OFFICES) can give you the latest information on tours and package holidays.

Some charter flights are currently offered to Johannesburg, but you must reserve far ahead as space fills up quickly.

When to Go

The seasons, of course, are upside-down south of the Equator: July is mid-winter and Christmas can be hot. But the climate of South Africa is mostly temperate. Summer is the rainy season in much of the country, though generally it's a matter of a passing thunderstorm to relieve the heat. (An exception is the Mediterranean-style Western Cape, which is dry all summer with rain in the winter.) On the Natal coast, the Indian Ocean is swimmable year-round.

At Kruger National Park, the game-spotting is easiest in winter—from July to October. Because it's dry then, the winter foliage affords less camouflage to animals looking for water-holes.

Average monthly temperatures for Cape Town and Johannesburg:

		J	F	M	A	M	J	J	A	S	O	N	D
Cape Town													
Max.	°F	79	80	79	74	68	64	63	64	66	70	75	77
	°C	26	27	26	23	20	18	17	18	19	21	24	25
Min.	°F	61	61	59	55	52	48	46	48	50	54	57	59
	°C	16	16	15	13	11	9	8	9	10	12	14	15
Johannesburg													
Max.	°F	79	79	75	72	66	61	61	68	74	77	77	79
	°C	26	26	24	22	19	16	16	20	23	25	25	26
Min.	°F	57	55	55	50	45	39	39	43	48	54	55	57
	°C	14	13	13	10	7	4	4	6	9	12	13	14

Planning Your Budget

The following are some prices in South African rands (R). However, they must be regarded as *approximate;* inflation is a factor in South Africa as elsewhere.

Airport transfers. SAA bus from Jan Smuts Airport to central Johannesburg R 13.60, to Pretoria R 15, taxi to central Johannesburg R 50–60.

Air travel. Scheduled jet Johannesburg–Cape Town (one way) R 428, Johannesburg–Durban R 229.

Car hire (international company). *VW Golf* R 80 per day plus 80c per km., or R 108 per day plus 80c per km., plus 300 km. free mileage (minimum rental seven days). *Microbus* R 350 per day plus R 2.20 per km., plus 300 km. free mileage (minimum seven days). Prices do not include insurance.

Cigarettes. R 2.50 per packet of 20, R 3.50 per packet of 30.

Excursions. Full-day Cape Peninsula tour from Cape Town R 105, three-day Johannesburg–Kruger Park coach tour including accommodation (shared room, per person) R 770, three-day Johannesburg–Sun City coach tour including accommodation, double room R 450 per person, single room R 550.

Hairdressers. *Man's* haircut R 12–20. *Woman's* haircut R 25–30, shampoo and set R 30–35, blow-dry R 25–30.

Hotels (double room with bath). ***** R 250, *** R 125 with breakfast, * R 40–50 with breakfast.

Meals and drinks (medium-priced restaurant). Lunch R 20–25, dinner R 30–45, bottle of wine R 15, beer R 2.50–3.50, brandy R 2–2.50, imported whisky R 2–2.50, soft drink R 1.50–2.50.

Taxis. Fares vary from town to town. Meters start at about R 3, plus R 1.50 per km.

Trains (one-way ticket). Johannesburg–Cape Town, *Blue Train,* standard compartment (per person, meals included) R 1200, Johannesburg–Pretoria R 8.50.

An A–Z Summary of Practical Information and Facts

> A star (*) following an entry indicates that relevant prices are to be found on page 109.

A

ACCOMMODATION*. See also CAMPING. The South African Hotel Board rates hotels with stars—five for the top standard of luxury, one for the simple comforts. At the five-star level, all the smart extras are supplied: swimming pool, tennis courts, sauna, choice of restaurants and bars, and, of course, air-conditioning throughout. The prices rise to international standards, too. More surprising is the degree of comfort of hotels at the bottom end of the scale. Many two-star establishments, for instance, have spacious air-conditioned rooms, and one-star hotels have a high percentage of rooms with private baths. All the hotels approved by the Board maintain a high standard; most are good value for money.

The South African Tourist Corporation (Satour) publishes an annual directory of hotels, motels, rest camps in game parks, caravan and campsites, rooming houses, beach cottages and holiday flats and bungalows for the whole country. It's incomparably useful either for planning far ahead or for last-minute use on arrival wherever you're touring. Accommodation is normally heavily booked for the South African school holiday periods (December/January, the Easter period, June/July and October), but at other times there should be no problem. On the contrary, many establishments offer off-season reduced prices.

Among many other details, the Satour hotel directory reports the status of every establishment's liquor licence (if any), the policy on pets, whether there is access for the physically handicapped, and finally the price scale. Because of inflation, the latter specification may be sadly outdated. Note that all prices include VAT at the standard rate of 10%. Telephone service will be charged extra.

Youth hostels. For full information, ask for the brochure issued by the South African Youth Hostels Association (also available at offices of Satour). Y.M.C.A. and Y.W.C.A. hostels are found in the cities, but they are more expensive than the youth hostels.

South African Youth Hostels Association, P.O. Box 4402, Cape Town 8000; tel. (021) 419-1853.

AIRPORTS*. South Africa's principal airport, Jan Smuts International, is about 30 kilometres from Johannesburg and 60 kilometres from Pretoria. Its main runway can handle any passenger jet fully loaded for an intercontinental voyage.

Services in the modern terminal: restaurants and bars, shops, hairdresser, pharmacy, florist, post office, bank, insurance and car-hire desks, airline club lounges, duty-free shop.

Metered taxis are available. An airport bus runs to and from the SAA terminal opposite Johannesburg main railway station (called the Rotunda), a trip of about half an hour:

Airport to city centre: every 30 min. from 6.15 a.m. to 11 p.m.
City centre to airport: every 30 min. from 5.30 a.m. to 10 p.m.

There's also a coach service to and from Pretoria (returning from the city SAA terminal about 2 hours before flight departure).

Two other South African airports are also classified as international: Durban's Louis Botha (about 20 km. south-west of the city; bus service to the SAA town terminal) and Cape Town's D.F. Malan (21 km. south-east of the city; bus service to the railway station). But the great bulk of their traffic is on domestic routes.

South African Airways runs several flights a day linking these cities with Port Elizabeth, East London, Kimberley and Bloemfontein and smaller centres. Private airlines supplement with flights to other towns and to Kruger National Park.

BABY-SITTERS*. Hotels routinely solve this problem, though the fees can vary from place to place. In Johannesburg, you can dial:

The Babysitter at (011) 802-2912.

CAMPING and CARAVANNING. Good weather and good roads account for the popularity of camping and caravanning in South Africa. There are about 650 caravan (trailer) parks around the country, often in perfectly beautiful surroundings; many of them have tent sites and amenities for campers, as well. Facilities at most caravan parks are relatively lavish: hot and cold showers and bathrooms, laundries, rooms for ironing clothes and washing dishes, and, in some cases, swimming pools, recreational halls, restaurants and shops. Popular parks, especially near the beaches, are likely to be full from mid-December to mid-January and at Easter.

You can rent a caravan and the car to tow it, or, less widely available, a self-contained motor caravan (camper). They come fully equipped with linen, kitchen utensils, stoves and refrigerators.

C Although rented cars can usually be picked up in one city and returned in another, caravans must go back to the point of hire if a collection charge is to be avoided.

For hikers, a series of trails is being developed; eventually it's to reach from the mountains of the Cape to the northern Transvaal. General information, and addresses to write to for maps and details of individual trails, are contained in the booklet *Follow the Footprints*, available from Satour, the South African Tourist Corporation, and its overseas offices (see TOURIST INFORMATION OFFICES).

CAR HIRE*. See also DRIVING. The well-known international car-hire firms have offices at airports, in all the big cities and even in small towns throughout South Africa. There are also local companies, which usually offer slightly lower tariffs. The cars available, normally Japanese or German makes, begin with two-door compacts and escalate to full-fledged limousines. Vans may also be hired. All vehicles come equipped with radios, some with air-conditioning.

The standard international conditions prevail in South Africa: the renter must have a valid driver's licence; usually a minimum age is specified—23 or 25. A cash deposit may be required, except where recognized credit cards are used for payment. The rates include basic insurance, but collision damage waiver and personal accident insurance are optional extras. Fuel is not included in the rate.

Chauffeur-driven cars are also available through some of the companies, the rates increasing with the size of the car.

CIGARETTES, CIGARS, TOBACCO*. Familiar British and American brands of cigarettes are manufactured under licence in South Africa; there are also local makes, usually with American-sounding names. By British and American standards, the prices are low. Cigars and pipe tobacco may be found in tobacconist shops and in some cafés (general stores). Regulations on smoking in public vary from city to city but are generally not too pervasive, and in any case, observance of the rules is haphazard.

CLIMATE and CLOTHING. If you arrive from the northern hemisphere's winter, you may be startled to see customs men at the airport in Johannesburg wearing short trousers. And businessmen as well. But even in the hottest South African summer, a degree of formality is appropriate after dark. A medium-priced hotel in Durban sums up its rules: "Gentlemen are requested to wear long trousers to dinner. Beachwear is not acceptable at any time in the restaurant." In the more exclusive hotels and restaurants, jackets and ties are highly recommended, though not totally obligatory.

In the game parks, at holiday resorts and while you're in transit, very casual clothing suffices. Fancy safari suits are quite unnecessary at Kruger National Park; anything comfortable will do.

For South African summer, pack lightweight clothing, but a light jacket or sweater for the occasional chilly evening. A raincoat or umbrella would be useful. The rest of the year, warm clothing will be required after dark, though daytime temperatures are often delightful. If you're going to the Indian Ocean coast, don't forget a bathing suit at any time of year.

COMMUNICATIONS

Post office. Most post offices are open from 8.30 a.m. to 4.30 p.m. Monday to Friday and 8 a.m. to noon on Saturdays. The smaller offices close for lunch from 1 to 2 p.m.

As in Britain, they deal with a complicated variety of business, from TV licences to pensions, so you may have to wait a bit for your postage stamp. Mail boxes, many of them bearing the monograms of British sovereigns, are painted bright red. Service is reasonably fast on overseas mail.

Poste restante. If you aren't sure where you'll be staying, you may have mail addressed to you Poste Restante (general delivery). The main post offices—on Parliament Street in Cape Town, West Street in Durban, Jeppe Street in Johannesburg—have special counters for this service.

Telegrams. The post office handles electronic communications as well. Any branch office will accept your telegram. The main post offices in Johannesburg and Cape Town have a cable and telegraph counter available 24 hours a day.

Telephone. South Africa's automatic telephone network functions as well as most in Europe or North America, and you can dial direct to many countries overseas. Local calls are cheaper between 9 p.m. and 7 a.m. from Monday to Saturday and between 1 p.m. on Saturday and 7 a.m. on Monday.

In Johannesburg, an international telephone office on the ground floor of the Post Office building in Smal Street stays open 24 hours a day.

For local calls, there are coin-operated telephones in street boxes and in cafés and public places. The complicated directions for use are posted in English and Afrikaans.

C **CONVERTER CHARTS.** For fluid and distance measures, see pp. 116–117. South Africa has long since abandoned acres and pints for hectares and litres. A quick reference service for non-metric-speakers:

Temperature

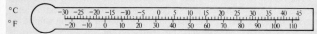

Length

Weight

CRIME and THEFT. As in most of the world, burglaries and muggings are becoming commonplace in South African cities. It makes sense to lock your property out of sight in the boot of your car, and lock the doors, too. Use the hotel safe for any valuables. And don't go out flashing jewellery or otherwise inviting trouble.

But there's one place where crime seems unheard of: the huts at Kruger National Park have no locks on the doors.

CUSTOMS and ENTRY REGULATIONS. Citizens of most countries require South African visas in addition to valid passports. To obtain a visa, which is issued free of charge, you should apply in person at the nearest South African diplomatic office, or by mail to the Director General, Home Affairs:

Private Bag X114, Pretoria 0001, South Africa

Allow plenty of time for the lengthy application form to be processed. If you plan to include a visit to any of the neighbouring countries and then return to South Africa, include this information on your application so you will receive a multiple-entry visa. (To drive from Durban to East London, for instance, you would have to pass through the Transkei and re-enter South Africa.)

On the plane, you'll be given another long form to fill in. Present this to the Passport Control Officer upon arrival in South Africa. This is the man who finally issues every visitor a temporary residence permit specifying the length and purpose of the stay. You have to convince this officer that you can support yourself in South Africa, and if you don't have a return ticket you must show that you have the means to buy one.

Here are the main items you may take into South Africa duty-free and, upon your return home, into your own country:

Into:	Cigarettes	Cigars	Tobacco	Spirits	Wine
S. Africa	400 and	50	and 250 g.	1 l. and	2 l.
Australia	200 or	250 g. or	250 g.	1 l. or	1 l.
Canada	200 and	50	and 900 g.	1.1 l. or	1.1 l.
Eire	200 or	50	or 250 g.	1 l. and	2 l.
N. Zealand	200 or	50	or 250 g.	1.1 l. and	4.5 l.
U.K.	200 or	50	or 250 g.	1 l. and	2 l.
U.S.A.	200 and	100	and *	1 l. or	1 l.

*A reasonable quantity.

Currency restrictions. Tourists may bring limitless amounts of foreign currency (preferably as traveller's cheques) into South Africa provided they are declared upon arrival—but note any restrictions on exporting cash from your own country. The amount of South African Reserve Bank notes you may carry into or out of South Africa is limited to R 200.

DRIVING IN SOUTH AFRICA. With 45,000 kilometres of paved roads and some 1,400 kilometres of dual carriageway (divided highway), South Africa is in good shape to invite tourists to see the country by car.

Paper work. You must have a valid driving licence with your photo and signature attached, and the details printed in English, or an accompanying certificate of authenticity in English. Or an international

D licence, obtained before your departure. If you plan to rent a car in South Africa, there are no unusual requirements (see CAR HIRE), but if you plan to import your car, advance planning and documentation are complicated. For details, consult Satour (see TOURIST INFORMATION OFFICES) or the Automobile Association of South Africa:

66 De Korte Street, Braamfontein, Johannesburg 2001
(tel. (011) 407-1000 or 0-800-111-999 (toll-free)

Driving conditions. Because of the British legacy, South Africa drives on the left. If you're not accustomed to it, start slowly and be especially vigilant when making turns. The speed limit on motorways (expressways) is 120 kilometres per hour. Elsewhere, 100 k.p.h. but generally 60 k.p.h. in built-up areas unless otherwise posted. In rural areas be careful of animals and pedestrians on the roads.

Distance

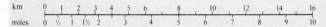

Road signs. Standard international pictographs are used for most situations, but there are some South African peculiarities. All printed signs are bilingual, e.g., "Border/Grens" or "Ompad/Detour". Or else they alternate, so you must remember that Kaapstad means Cape Town and is not some new destination suddenly revealed. But there is no town named Slegs. The frequently seen sign "Slegs Only" with an arrow turning, merely means the lane in question must be used for turning. (*Only* is *slegs* in Afrikaans.) Restrictions on parking are indicated by letters in circles painted on the road surface. An encircled L means loading zone (goods vehicles only); B means reserved for buses, T for taxis and FB for fire-fighting equipment. An S with a diagonal stripe means no stopping, a striped P is a no-parking indicator. Traffic lights are called "robots", a word needing no translation in English or Afrikaans.

Law enforcement. You'll rarely see a police patrol car on a South African highway. This is said to be one explanation for the heavy road toll—South Africa has one of the highest accident rates in the world. But if your luck runs out, fines for minor offences may be paid on the spot.

Fuel. Filling stations are found on all the main roads, though in country areas they're widely dispersed. Most stations are open only between 7 a.m. and 7 p.m. Monday to Saturday, but every town has one or more stations open beyond these hours. Grades of fuel available are 93 and 97 octane. Most stations offer full service, even after hours, and attendants routinely clean the windscreen and check oil and water.

Fluid measures

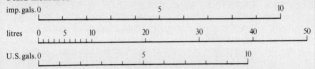

Driving in the Kruger National Park. The park is geared to the age of the motor car. There are about 900 kilometres of tarred roads in the park, plus 1,500 kilometres of gravel roads. Speed limits—very low—are posted. Slow driving gives the animal pedestrians a better chance of survival; additionally, you are more likely to sight game in the bush at 20 k.p.h. than at 40.

Though some purists prefer the wilderness feeling of the back roads, the well-surfaced roads have their advantages. They are dust-less and much more comfortable. The animals, who may be seen alongside all kinds of road, have no strong feelings. But they prefer to eat the dust-free vegetation along the tarred roads.

The animals consider the cars just another species of wild-life. If you step out of your car—even if you stick your head or arms out the window—it changes you into a recognizable human, frightening some kinds of animals and prompting others to attack. This is why you are required to stay inside the car anywhere beyond the fenced camps, barring an emergency. The authorities emphasize that there are no tame animals in the Kruger Park, not even the lovable-looking vervet monkeys, which may bite. Feeding any animal is strictly forbidden.

Some more regulations: you may not drive off an authorized road—into the bush or onto a road with a "no entry" sign. Among other dangers, if your car should break down in an unauthorized place, help might not reach you for days. You may not bring firearms into the park unless they are declared and sealed at the gate. And no pets are allowed.

One rule which is taken very seriously is the closing of the gates. In winter you must be back in your camp, or out of the park, by 5.30 p.m., in summer by 6.30. If you're five minutes late you'll be locked out and subject to a fine. The excuse that the road was blocked by elephants has been invented so often that it is no longer accepted, even

D when true. Night travel is forbidden in the park to protect the animals and also to make life more difficult for poachers. For bookings for the park within South Africa, ring the National Parks Board in Pretoria; tel. (012) 343-1991.

E **ELECTRIC CURRENT.** Although the voltage varies slightly from one city to another, current is generally 220 volts A.C., 50 cycles. Hardware stores and supermarkets provide adaptor plugs for electric razors and appliances to fit the outlets in some hotels. South Africa still has the round three-pin plugs, as opposed to the square ones.

EMBASSIES and CONSULATES. See also the yellow pages of local telephone directories under "Consulates and Embassies".

Australia	Mutual and Federal Building, 220 Vermeulen St., Pretoria; tel. (012) 325-4315 14th floor, B.P. Centre, Long St., Cape Town; tel. (021) 419-5425
Canada	Nedbank Plaza, Church and Beatrix streets, Arcadia, Pretoria; tel. (012) 28-7062
Eire	London House, 21 Loveday St., Johannesburg; tel. (011) 836-5869
United Kingdom	255 Hill St., Arcadia, Pretoria; tel. (012) 43-3121 91 Parliament St., Cape Town; tel. (021) 25-3670 19th floor, Sanlau Centre, Jeppe St., Johannesburg; tel. (011) 337-8940 10th floor, Fedlife House, 320 Smith St., Durban; tel. (031) 305-2929
U.S.A.	Thibault House, Pretoria St., Pretoria; tel. (012) 28-4266 Broadway Industries Centre, Cape Town; tel. (021) 21-4280 11th floor, Kine Centre, Commissioner St., Johannesburg; tel. (011) 331-1681 Durban Bay House, 333 Smith St., Durban; tel. (031) 304-4737

EMERGENCIES. In Johannesburg, Cape Town and Durban, the police flying squad answers emergency calls at 1-0111.

	Ambulance	Fire
Johannesburg	1-0177	331-2222
Cape Town	1-0177	461-5555
Durban	1-0177	309-3333

GUIDES and INTERPRETERS. Package tours of Kruger National
Park are led by experienced guides who can help spot the animals and
identify them. In the private game parks, rangers are able to give
attention to visitors' individual interests, such as bird watching. City
sightseeing tours and day excursions to beauty spots are normally hand-
led by bilingual (English and Afrikaans) guides. For interpreters of
other languages, check with the local tourist office.

HEALTH and MEDICAL CARE

Vaccinations. Smallbox and cholera vaccinations are no longer required
for entry into South Africa but anti-malaria tablets should be taken.
Anyone arriving in South Africa from a yellow fever zone must have a
valid international yellow fever vaccination certificate.

Malaria tablets should be taken by everyone planning to visit Kruger
National Park or the private game parks nearby. Ask your pharmacist
or doctor to explain the precautions you must take. Or you can go to
any pharmacy in South Africa and buy anti-malaria pills over the
counter. Normally you must start taking the pills several days before
entering the affected district and continue the specified dosage for
several weeks after leaving. A syrup is made for children's use.

Problems. Aside from sharks, "bluebottles" (men-of war) and tides,
ocean swimming presents no special problems. However, be extremely
careful about rivers and lakes: unless otherwise announced, they may
be inhabited by the dangerous bilharzia parasite, contracted by ingest-
ing unpurified water or through bare feet or skin in or near the water.
Never drink from a river unless you've been assured it is potable.

Most of the 140 varieties of snakes inhabiting South Africa are
harmless, or almost. But if the worst happens, anti-snake-bite serum is
available.

Insurance. Since South Africa has no national health service, any
medical treatment and hospitalization must be paid for direct. If you
have medical insurance already, make quite certain that it covers foreign countries. You may prefer, however, to keep on the safe side and

119

H take out special travel insurance to cover accident, illness or hospitalization on your trip.

Doctors. Most hotels have a list of nearby doctors in case of need. Or look in the white pages of the telephone directory under "Medise Praktisyns" or "Medical Practitioners". Dentist are listed under "Tandartse"/"Dentists".

Hospitals. All cities have well-equipped hospital faciltes, some of international repute.

Pharmacies. In the big cities, one shop in each area stays open after normal business hours. Check in the local newspaper for details of late opening hours.

HOURS. See also COMMUNICATIONS and MONEY MATTERS. Most **shops** stay open from 8.30 a.m. to 5 p.m. Monday to Friday and until 1 p.m. on Saturdays. Certain types of shop–greengrocers, pharmacies, bookshops and some supermarkets—stay open later. Cafés (essentially small general stores) may operate from 6 a.m. to midnight seven days a week. Some big shopping centres stay open till 5 p.m. on Saturdays and from 9 a.m. to 1 p.m. on Sundays. Beachfront shops of all kinds in Durban stay open all day on Sundays.

Cango Caves, Oudtshoorn: December, January, February, April, tours for visitors every hour from 8 a.m. to 5 p.m., off season every second hour from 9 a.m. to 3 p.m.

Kruger National Park opens from 5 a.m. to 6.30 p.m. in summer and 6.30 a.m. to 5.30 p.m. in winter.

Premier Diamond Mine, Cullinan: tours at 9.30 Tuesday to Friday (not for children under 10). Tour takes 8 hours.

State Opera and theatre complex, Pretoria: guided tours at 11 a.m. Monday, Wednesday and Friday and at 4.30 p.m. on Wednesdays.

Stock Exchange, Johannesburg: guided tours at 11 a.m. and 2.30 p.m. Monday to Friday.

Voortrekker Monument, Pretoria: 9 a.m.–4.45 p.m. Monday and Wednesday to Saturday and 2–4.45 p.m. on Sundays but closed on Good Friday and Christmas Day.

L **LANGUAGE.** In polyglot South Africa, the blacks speak nine principal languages, the Asians, six; the official languages are English and Afrikaans. Most of the whites and "coloureds" (people of mixed race) claim Afrikaans as their mother tongue. Afrikaans is about as close to Dutch as Portuguese is to Spanish. In practice, you'll almost never meet anyone who doesn't understand English. But here are a few phrases you might try in an Afrikaans environment (note that the "g" is pronounced "kh").

Good morning	**Goeie môre**
Good afternoon	**Goeie middag**
Good night	**Goeie nag**
Please	**Asseblief**
Thank you	**Dankie**
Goodbye	**Tot siens**

Here are some distinctive words in everyday use by both English and Afrikaans speakers in South Africa:

bakkie	pickup truck	**rondavel**	circular house
braai	barbecue	**verkrampte**	bigoted,
outspan	break a journey		narrow-minded
"robot"	traffic light	**verligte**	broadminded

LAUNDRY and DRY-CLEANING. Hotels offer good, fast service, often returning the clothing the same day when requested. In the towns, there are commercial laundries and dry-cleaning establishments as well as self-service launderettes (where you can also leave a load of washing and pick it up later, dried and folded).

MAPS. The South African Tourist Corporation (Satour) issues (free) first-class tourist maps of South Africa and the regions. Local tourist offices, car-hire firms and the Automobile Association (for AA members) also are sources of free maps. Extremely detailed, indexed maps of cities and regions are sold at bookstores.

MEETING PEOPLE. The South Africans are more friendly and open than most, so there's no problem about striking up a conversation anywhere—in a bus or supermarket, on a beach or on safari. Because of the adverse publicity the country receives in most of the world, you'll find South Africans unusually sensitive to the views of foreigners, so it's wise not to overstate any political opinions.

Be aware of the delicacies you might encounter because of racial or religious differences. For instance, if you visit a mosque, you must leave your shoes outside. If you want to take pictures of black tribal dances, first determine whether there are any objections.

M MONEY MATTERS

Currency. The unit of currency of South Africa is the rand (abbreviated R), divided into 100 cents (c).

Coins: 1, 2, 5, 10, 20, 50c, R 1 and R 2

Banknotes: R 5, 10, 20, 50

For currency restrictions, see CUSTOMS AND ENTRY REGULATIONS.

Banking hours. 9 a.m.–3.30 p.m. Monday to Friday, 8.30–11 a.m. on Saturdays (later in the major cities). Small-town banks close for lunch from 12.45 to 2 p.m. (except on Wednesdays and Saturdays).

Credit Cards and Traveller's Cheques. All commercial banks cash traveller's cheques provided they are in a currency accepted in South Africa. Many hotels and shops also accept traveller's cheques. Internationally-known credit cards are recognized in most hotels, tourist-orientated shops, and by tour operators and carriers.

Taxes. Since the latter part of 1991, the tax system has changed to VAT at a standard rate of 10%, except on some basic foodstuffs. This means that the price you see is the VAT-inclusive price you pay.

N NEWSPAPERS and MAGAZINES.

English-language dailies, published in all the main cities of South Africa, carry national and international news and syndicated features. In the main centres, British newspapers may be found—a bit late and extremely expensive because of air freight charges. The major American newsmagazines are sold everywhere, and some newsagents also carry British, German, French and Italian magazines. Certain books and magazines are prohibited for moral or ideological reasons.

P PHOTOGRAPHY.

Because of sanctions, which cover also foreign makes of films, you'll need to bring your own or buy locally made films. Same day processing is available in most cities and larger resorts. Keep your film as cool as possible in the semi-tropical regions. Never leave your camera locked in a car parked in the hot sun.

Before you leave on holiday, be sure your camera is in perfect condition. Change the batteries. If you've just bought a new camera, learn all about it and take some test pictures before you leave home. If your equipment is expensive, insure it.

Shooting animals in the game park requires fast film—ASA 200—because the subject may move, and so may your long lens. However, a telephoto lens is by no means essential. Many animals come so close that the cheapest amateur camera could serve the purpose.

Some airport security machines use X-rays which can ruin your film. Ask that it be checked separately, or enclose it in a lead-lined bag.

POLICE. Members of South Africa's national police force, who are armed, wear safari-suit uniforms and peaked caps. In the cities they usually drive small "Black Maria" vans (actually yellow) with caged space for culprits in the rear. On the highways, patrol cars of the traffic police are rarely seen.

PUBLIC HOLIDAYS

January 1	New Year's Day
April 6	Founder's Day
May 1	Labour Day
May 31	Republic Day
October 10	Kruger Day
December 16	Day of the Vow
December 25	Christmas Day
December 26	Day of Goodwill

Movable Dates:
Good Friday, Family Day (Easter Monday), Ascension Day.

RADIO and TV. The South African Broadcasting Corporation transmits three principal services on FM: the English Service, patterned after BBC Radio Four, with old-fashioned BBC accents maintained; the Afrikaans Service; and Radio 5, specializing in broadcasts of pop music. In addition, three are regional services, strong on pop music, on AM and FM. "702" is an independent music-news radio station. BBC, Voice of America and European shortwave stations can be picked up in South Africa; BBC and VOA also use a medium-wave frequency for southern Africa, morning and night.

The English/Afrikaans television channel, TV1, divides the evenings equally between the official languages. CCTV, formerly TV2 and 3, broadcast in English and African languages. M-Net is a popular cable TV station, received throughout South Africa.

R **RELIGIOUS SERVICES.** South Africans belong to 22 organized denominations and five main faiths. The largest congregation is the Dutch Reformed church, followed by the Anglican and Roman Catholic churches. The Great Synagogue in Cape Town is called the oldest in the southern hemisphere. For details of all religious services, see the Saturday editions of local newspapers.

T **TIME DIFFERENCES.** All year round, South Africa keeps two hours ahead of Greenwich Mean Time. In European winter, the differences look this way:

Los Angeles	New York	London	**South Africa**	Sydney
2 a.m.	5 a.m.	10 a.m.	**noon**	9 p.m.

TIPPING. In South Africa, tipping is neither as widespread nor as generous as in most of Europe and North America. Tips are awaited, but not always received, by filling station attendants, hotel maids, railway porters, taxi drivers, waiters, stewards and caddies.

Some suggestions:

Barber/Hairdresser	10% (minimum)
Maid, per week	R 15–20
Porter, per bag	R 2.50
Taxi driver	10%
Tourist guide	10%
Waiter	10% if service charge not included

TOILETS. Public conveniences are well signposted in the centre of many towns. They are usually segregated by race as well as gender, so watch the signs. Hotels, restaurants and big department stores are usually good bets for clean facilities elsewhere.

TOURIST INFORMATION OFFICES. About 50 South African cities and towns have Publicity Associations or similar autonomous organizations for the benefit of visiting tourists. They issue pamphlets and maps and dispense free advice and often help with hotel reservations. Some of the big ones:

Johannesburg Publicity Association, Northstate Building, corner Market and Kruis streets, P.O. Box 4580, Johannesburg 2000; 24-hour tourist information service. Phone (011) 29-4961 (office hours), 402-5000 (after hours).

Pretoria Visitor's Information Bureau, Munitoria Building, corner Vermeulen and Van der Walt streets; tel. (012) 313-7980.

Durban Publicity Association and Visitors' Bureau, West Street, corner of Church Street; tel. (031) 304-4934/4981. 24-hour Teletourist (031) 305-2723.

Cape Town Tourism Authority (Captour), 14 Strand Concourse, Adderley Street, Cape Town; tel. (021) 25-3320.

Each major centre will also have a National Tourist Bureau (NTB), that is able to provide countrywide information.

South African Tourism Board (Satour), head office:

Menlyn Park Office Block, Atterbury Road and Menlyn Drive, Menlyn 0081; tel. (012) 347-0600; fax (012) 47-1676.

Postal address: Private Bag X164, Pretoria 0001.

Satour offices abroad:

United Kingdom	Regency House, 1–4 Warwick Street, London W1R 5WB; tel. 439-9661
U.S.A.	747 Third Avenue, New York, NY 10017; tel. 838-8841 Suite 1524, 9841 Airport Boulevard, Los Angeles, CA; tel. (213) 641-8444
Australia	SAA offices, 5 Elizabeth Street, Sydney 2000; tel. 233-6855 SAA offices, Exchange House, 68 St George's Terrace, Perth 8000; tel. 322-7388
Germany	Ale Manniahaus, An der Hauptwache 11, Postfach 101940, D-6 Frankfurt/Main 1; tel. (069) 20656
Italy	Via M. Gonzaga, 3, Milano 20123; tel. (02) 8693847, 8793847

T	**Japan**	Akasaka Lions Building, 1-1-2 Moto, Akasaka, Minato-ku, Tokyo 107; tel. 478-7601
	Netherlands	Parnassustoren, Locatellikade 1, 1076 AZ, Amsterdam; tel. 664-6201
	Switzerland	Seestrasse 42, CH-8802 Kilchberg, Zürich; tel. (01) 715 18156/7

TRANSPORT

Buses. In Johannesburg, the Publicity Association sells reduced-rate tickets for unlimited bus travel except on peak-hour buses. Bus route-maps and timetables are also sold at the City Hall, Market Street. Evening bus services are sparse, and from 2 p.m. Saturday to Monday morning all municipal buses depart from the station at Main and Rissik streets.

Other cities have bus services of less complexity. Information is offered at local tourist information offices. In all buses, even the double-deckers, you pay the driver on the way in. Keep your ticket, for an inspector is likely to board the bus to double-check.

Taxis*. In South African cities the taxis do not normally cruise for fares. You must go to a taxi rank or have your hotel desk clerk summon a cab by phone. In Johannesburg taxis are usually found outside the Carlton Centre in Kruis Street. In Cape Town a likely taxi rank is opposite the Air Terminal in Lower Adderley Street.

Trains*. One way or another, many South African trains are fascinating. There are 1,600 steam locomotives still earning their keep—a rare thrill for train buffs. Several narrow-gauge lines still operate; the best known is the route from Port Elizabeth to Avontuur—285 kilometres of 2'0" gauge railway. At the other end of the scale, the Blue Train (see p. 90), the pride of South African Railways, maintains five-star luxury between Pretoria and Cape Town. Other luxury trains link Johannesburg, Durban and Cape Town. All long-distance trains have sleeping compartments in first and second class. Workaday commuter trains are a less glamorous story.

W **WATER.** All over South Africa you can drink the water from the tap—even in your hut in the Kruger National Park. In some coastal areas the water comes out an unappetizing colour because of iron
deposits, but it's still potable.

Index

An asterisk (*) next to a page number indicates a map reference.